TRUE PSYCHOLOGY

A Scientific Approach to a Better Life

TRUE PSYCHOLOGY

A Scientific Approach to a Better Life

DR. GALEN E. COLE

Aphalon Firth, an imprint of
Aphalon Firth Publishing Company

CONTENTS

CONTENTS

CONTENTS

CONTENTS

CONTENTS

PREFACE AND DEDICATIONS

For some strange reason, I believe it was fate, I had more than my fair share of problems growing up, including the death of my brother when I was a teenager. Fortunately, through all of my difficulties I do not recollect thinking my life was that much different or more difficult than the lives of those I grew up around.

What I do recall about my many struggles is my relentless desire to see the good in everything I was experiencing. That is, I was an optimist. This is probably because those I grew up around were some of the most pessimistic people I have ever known. For example, I recall asking my dad if he would help me pay for college. His answer was, "No, you really aren't college material, you need to learn to do something with your hands!" It was at that moment, in spite of the fact that I struggled in school and the only reason I did reasonably well was to remain eligible for sports, I decided I was going to go to college. After all, the true optimist performs best in the presence of a true pessimist. And my dad was a true pessimist. No wonder, given that he grew up in a very difficult world filled with poverty and disappointments—disappointments that only gave way to alcohol until the point in time when he learned, internalized, and began to apply the principles outlined in this book.

One problem with being a true optimist is the fact that, in spite of a positive outlook on life, bad things happen that can shake this sense of optimism to the core. This is especially true when bad things happen over and over again. For example, during my senior year in high school I lost the state championship in wrestling in the last two seconds of the match. And then, in college, I lost a deciding match to the national champion in my weight class in the last few seconds of the match on a technicality. Because I spent my growing up years dreaming of being a state and national champion, these losses caused me to rethink my optimism. What I discovered in this time of deep reflection is the substance of this book, which has been repeated over and over again across my life span.

The most important underlying assumption that supports my theory of self-improvement states that, "In case of happiness and emotional well-being, it is not what happens to a person, but what the person decides to think and do about what happens to him or her that counts." Ironically, when I decided to write this book in 2012, this theory was severely challenged by the deaths of my mother on March 5, 2012, my grandmother on my birthday, March 17, 2012, and my mother's brother on March 24, 2012. In keeping with what you will learn from the book, each one of these crushing losses presented me with an opportunity to become better or bitter, stronger or weaker, more or less rational. And in each instance, I made a conscious decision to become better, stronger, and more rational.

If applied as prescribed, the "True Psychology" approach presented here will teach you how to consistently choose to use the inevitable difficulties and problems you experience in life, small or large, as opportunities for personal and interpersonal growth and development. I have not discovered a new drug, supplement, or secret treatment. Instead, I provide principles that allow insight into the human condition that can improve one person at a time. The book will also help you clearly see the truth in the common laymen's definition of insanity, which is "doing the same thing over and over again while expecting a different outcome."

By using the words "True Psychology" in the title of this book, I assert that the principles discussed here can be applied at any time in any culture with the same outcome. I know this is a bold assertion, but it is true. And, what's more important, because these ideas are based on universal truths, you can test them on yourself, in your relationships with others, in your religious practice, and at work.

I refer to the principles and ideas asserted here as "universal truths" because they apply across cultures, time periods, races, and religions. For example, I discovered first-hand through my research and travels around the globe that individuals (regardless of their culture, race, or place of origin) who think negative thoughts or tell themselves irrational stories experience negative emotions. Similarly, those who consistently treat others with disrespect eventually lose the respect of those they mistreat.

If you think about it, it is truly a good thing that there are universal truths and laws that link human behavior to certain consequences. Once you learn universal laws and decide to comply with them, you can consistently reap the consequences associated with each law. This gives predictability and a sense of certainty and control over how our lives play out. This, in turn, gives us reassurance that life is not just a lottery or that we are simply preordained to a life that we have no control over. As any good parent or teacher or supervisor would readily say, "people tend to get out of life what they put into it." Or, put another way, they tend to "reap what they sow." As you will learn from this book, this includes how you feel as an individual as well as how you tend to relate to other people and organizations.

During my developmental years, I spent much of my time on a large cattle ranch. We knew when it was hot we needed to check the windmills each day to ensure the cattle had adequate water. Likewise, we knew in the winter time when the temperature dipped far below freezing we would need to break the ice in the water tanks to ensure that cattle could get a drink. And, if the snow covered all the pasture forage, we needed to supplement the cows' diet with hay. We knew that if we planted a garden we had to take certain steps to ensure that we reaped the benefits of our labors. We needed to till the ground, plant good seeds, fertilize, weed, water, and protect our crops from raccoons, coyotes, and deer. If we did this year after year, we always produced something that was edible.

I know this concept may seem somewhat elementary to the average adult, especially to those who have been around a while. However, many of those who have written about self-help psychology, and how it applies to individuals and their relationships, tend to leave out the part about the link between thoughts, behaviors, and consequences. This is certainly not true among those who have a true Cognitive Behavioral Therapy (CBT), Rational Emotive Behavior Therapy (REBT), and/or Dialectical Behavioral Therapy (DBT) perspective, but it is true among many others who put up a shingle and hope to help guide their clients toward good mental health and relationships. This is because many of the theories taught in graduate school are long on best guesses and short on common sense that in many cases must be learned through experience.

The principles, processes, and approaches outlined in this book are not simply theoretical fun and games. Rather, they are based on what leading behavioral and social scientists agree are the most important principles and conditions that must be addressed in an effective self-directed psychological change process.

More specifically, this means that learning and applying the true self-help psychology outlined here will help you achieve the following results: understand that everyone who has a healthy brain can learn to live rationally; appreciate the fact that healthy brains have the ability to change shape over time (neuroplasticity), which translates into desirable changes in the brain that result from conscious changes in thinking, i.e., you can use your mind to change your brain for the better; understand that rational living increases happiness and emotional well-being; learn to consistently perceive yourself in a way that increases your happiness and sense of well-being; think in ways that are congruent with rational goals and a rational perception of yourself and your future—a Rational Self-Perception (RSP); behave in ways that are consistent with rational goals and a RSP; develop realistic self-improvement plans that work; believe that, in case of happiness and emotional well-being, it is not what happens to you, or your circumstances, but what you decide to think and do about what happens to you and your circumstances that counts; form a strong positive intention (or make a commitment) to make specific changes; better understand what you can do to build personal resiliency and cope in healthy, rational ways; develop basics skills, including mental imagery and rehearsal, goal setting, resiliency development, coping, cognitive restructuring, critical thinking, self-discipline, delayed gratification, persistence, planning and problem solving; master monitoring personal status and internal monologues to align your thoughts with your goals; gain the confidence (self-efficacy) you need to do what is required to change; understand intrinsic and extrinsic motivation and how they impact goal-oriented thinking and action; develop positive reinforcement (motivation) for doing what you plan to do; understand how to identify your triggers and how to overcome your barriers and tendencies to self-sabotage; believe that the advantages of doing what you plan to do outweigh the disadvantages; ensure that what you plan to do and actually end up thinking and doing is, in fact, consistent with your self-image and does not violate your personal standards; understand that setting and striving toward specific goals will give you a greater sense that life has purpose and meaning and that achieving your personal goals will give you a discernible sense of accomplishment that is often referred to as success—the progressive realization of a worthy ideal. And, an appreciation for the fact that because setting and achieving goals gives an individual a sense of purpose and feelings of success, it is rational to set and achieve goals. Conversely, not setting goals, or setting goals that you do not achieve, is irrational. To be rational, a goal must specific, measurable, realistic, and stated in terms of a specific time period. In addition, you must believe you can achieve the goal (have self-efficacy or confidence) and actually be able to achieve it, i.e., have the required knowledge, skills, and abilities. This is because 1) it is irrational to assume you can achieve a goal that you do not believe you can achieve, and 2) you must become the kind of person who does the kind of thing you plan to do.

Once you understand these truths, you will know why people struggle as individuals and in their relationships. You will also know how to help yourself and others deal with even the most difficult problems in ways that make yourself, other individuals, and your relationships stronger. In other words, you will know how to consistently and systematically reprogram your beliefs, thoughts, actions, and perception in a way that helps you become the person you want to become, regardless of what happens to you across your life span.

To this end, I dedicate this book and the truths herein to the mostly unsung heroes across the world who receive so little credit for doing so much for all of us. This includes our fighting men and women, and especially my nephew Geoffrey Golden Johnson, who lost his life in Bagdad; police and firefighters like those individuals who charged into the Twin Towers, knowing that they may not come out again; helping professionals who spend countless hours trying to prevent suicide, emotional suffering, and divorce; individuals who turn their lives around and become happy and productive by overcoming crushing life events and the iron grip of addiction, like my father, Edward; public health professionals who tirelessly advocate for disease prevention and health promotion; and above all, mothers and teachers, who like my wife Priscilla, my mother Janice, and my grandmother Aurel, have strong agendas for good and devote themselves to socializing healthy, rational children against great odds and for little or no pay.

INTRODUCTION

I once received a call from a person who had a serious anxiety problem. He wanted to know how much I charged for psychotherapy. Before answering and in hopes of jarring some rational thinking into his decision-making process, I asked him if he had any other criteria for selecting a therapist besides price. He said, "Yes, I need someone who lives close to me." Even though I kindly suggested that he may want to ask a few more questions before making a final decision about who should help him with his problem, he continued to insist on finding the lowest priced and most conveniently located therapist. Realizing this person was not interested in the background, training, or experience of the person who would help him, I recommended that he go online and Google the phrase "cheapest therapists in Stone Mountain, Georgia" (his hometown).

Although I am not sure what he discovered, I do know that with such a limited selection criteria (cost and location), this person may have gone on to find a low-cost therapist, who has an office just around the corner, and who has absolutely no experience treating anxiety disorders. Just as not all therapists are the same, not all individuals who write "self-help books" are the same. I would hope that you keep this in mind as you look over my credentials and realize that what I have written here is not simply an exercise in theoretical fun and games. Rather, the ideas and recipes for change and personal development presented here are based on what leading behavioral and social scientists agree are the most important principles that must be included in any legitimate approach to helping people better themselves, overcome troubles, improve weaknesses, and ultimately lead happier, more serene, and healthier lives.

Since I can remember, I have had a passion for helping people. My wife claims I am trying to save the world. Although it took me a while to figure out how I was going to do it, I finally focused on two approaches that have served me well. The first "world saving" idea came to me when I took an undergraduate psychology class. When I learned that there was a profession where people would pay me to help them, I was hooked. I was even more intrigued when I took my first health science class and learned that there was a profession called public health that focused on preventing and controlling diseases among the population at large. After taking these two classes I decided I was going to get the credentials required to work in both counseling psychology and public health. This decision has served me well in that I have spent my professional life trying to change the world one person, couple, and family at a time in my clinics, and one community and country at a time through my work in public health.

In both of my professions I have spent a considerable amount of time training other like-minded professionals. This has taken me around the world to many exotic and wonderful places like Almaty, Kazakhstan; Abuja, Nigeria; Kampala, Uganda; Nairobi, Kenya; Nazareth, Israel; Cuzco, Peru; and Sidney, Australia.

The first time I really knew that I was having a broad-scale impact was at a training I was conducing in Bangkok, Thailand. After the training, some of the professionals who participated in my workshop asked me sit down for a special presentation. At that point they announced that a decision had been made to require all students in their last year of secondary school to use a synthetic learning support tool I was instrumental in developing, CDCynergy (Cole & Prue, 1999), to plan and evaluate their senior project. Not long after this experience I was in Beijing, China, introducing a similar synthetic learning and decision-support tool to the heads of the Chinese Centers for Disease Control—China CDC. Shortly after introducing my learning tool, my Chinese hosts started talking excitedly among themselves in Mandarin. After going back and forth for some time, they sent a person out of the room. Shortly afterwards, this person brought back a copy of the same tool I had planned to present to them. To my surprise and pleasure, the Chinese had somehow gotten a copy of my tool and translated it into Mandarin.

After recognizing that my work had reached as far as China, my passion and intensity to save the world has taken on even greater meaning and a dedication to reach as many people as I can. This has motivated me to reach out to, and begin working with, representatives of what I consider to be the most powerful channel for good or bad communication in the world, popular entertainment (Greenberg, Salmon, Patel, Beck & Cole, 2004). As you will read later in the book, my work with writers and producers in Hollywood has allowed me to influence millions with minimal effort. It has also taught me a number of principles that I have been able to incorporate into the psychology of self-directed change techniques I will introduce later in the book.

This book is another attempt at carrying out my global mission. The book brings together the collective wisdom I have assimilated through my experience in working with different cultures regarding 1) what it takes to motivate both individuals and large populations to eliminate unhealthy and irrational thoughts and actions and 2) how to replace them with attitudes and actions that produce rational living, increased health, happiness, and a state of serenity. In other words, it describes in some detail how "the psychology of change" can help individuals, couples, and families go about systematically improving themselves and their relationships. It also describes how those who are struggling with serious problems like addiction can overcome their cravings, remain sober, and become truly happy.

Seven quotes that I have discovered over the years have helped shape and guide my work to promote personal development and healthy relationships. Each of these quotes has impacted how I think about, approach, and promote the psychology of change and self-improvement.

The first quote is credited to Steven Covey. In fact, it is the title of the second chapter in his book 7 Habits of Highly Effective People. It simply says, "Begin with the end in mind." In keeping with this incredibly simple and, at the same time, incredibly important concept, Section I of this book provides an explanation of what I consider to be the end goal of the book, which is to persuade the reader that learning and applying the processes I introduce here, along with the accompanying psychology of change tools—taken from the fields of Cognitive Behavioral Therapy (CBT), Rational Emotive Behavior Therapy (REBT), and Dialectical Behavioral Therapy (DBT)—will help you identify and systematically go about attaining your personal algorithm for true happiness and well-being (Seligman, 2012; Rath & Hartner, 2010).

The second quote is a Turkish Proverb that says, "No matter how far you have gone on the wrong road, turn back." This quote reminds me to tell those I work with that they can, no matter how much havoc they have wreaked in their lives, change their course in life. It also reminds me to remind them that if they have gone down a wrong road for a long distance, it does take some time to get back to the right road. This truth is also evident in the next quote.

Jim Rohn states, "You cannot change your destination overnight, but you can change your direction overnight."

What this quote says to me is that a necessary first step in getting where you want to be is to make a decision to change your direction in life. Similar to the Turkish proverb I just discussed, this quote also reminds me that even though we do change course in life, it may take some time to get to our desired destination. Although individuals who do not value patience, an essential ingredient in true happiness, may not like the fact that change takes time and effort, the fact is, change does take time and effort.

The fourth quote that is fundamental to my philosophy of change is by Henry Louis Menken. "There is always a well-known solution to every human problem—neat, plausible, and wrong." This quote makes the point that change is not easy and that all those who say it is do not know what they are talking about, or they are manipulating the truth to make it seem like "change" is a magical process that requires no real dedication or effort.

The fifth quote I often rely upon is by Albert Einstein. "Make everything as simple as possible, but not simpler." As with the Menken quote, Einstein's point here is that making things too complicated can get in the way of the primary goal, which is to give people what they need to improve without overburdening them with details.

The sixth quote by Patrick Rothfuss, in the Name of the Wind, states, "It's like everyone tells a story about themselves inside their own head. Always. All the time. That story makes you what you are. We build ourselves out of that story." This quote makes the point that what we think about ourselves is crucial. No matter how hard we try to change, we cannot change in ways that are incongruent with our self-image. Because of this, any legitimate personal or interpersonal change or development process must target the self-image. This is why one of the steps in the self-directed process I introduce in Section IV focuses on changing the self-image.

The seventh quote I have relied on heavily in my efforts to help people improve their lives is attributed to Robert Louis Stevenson. He said, "No man can run away from weakness. He must either fight it out or perish. And if that be so . . . why not now, and where you stand." This reminds me to remind you that there is no time like the present to make changes that will help you overcome weakness on the road to greater happiness.

To summarize, the contents of this book represent a serious approach to psychological change, personal and interpersonal development, and recovery. Although there are many approaches to change, I believe my approach will provide you with a tried and true recipe for personal and interpersonal development and recovery. I say tried and true because the "recipes" presented here have been tested in my clinics and on large populations around the world and have proven to be universally effective. Again, by universal, I mean these principles have been effective in helping men, women, and children, of different races, from different cultures and religions, around the globe.

Section I "begins with the end in mind" by introducing

you to the end goal of the "Plan to Live Rationally" (P2LR) process explained in Section IV. This goal is quite simply to increase your happiness and serenity. This section explains what I mean by happiness and a sense of well-being. It also provides you with a straightforward exercise that you can use to begin the process of identifying your own unique "happiness recipe."

Section II explains and illustrates the concepts of "truth" and "rationality," in a way that will help you more readily understand and apply the process introduced in Section IV. The basic premise of this section is that without some understanding of (and a means of measuring) truth and rationality, it is impossible to make the case that the steps and stages that make up the P2LR process are any better or more effective than any other recipe for self- directed change.

What is described and illustrated in **Section III**, "Logic Models & Principles for Change," is presented here because I believe it is better to "teach a person to fish than it is to simply give a person a fish." Accordingly, an understanding of the models in Section III will help you understand, at a deep level, why the steps laid out in Section IV are both necessary and sufficient for change and development.

Section III also provides you with an extensive list of principles, assumptions, and conditions required to understand the scientific basis of psychological change and redirection. These ideas are what differentiate this approach from other self-help books that are not grounded in empirical evidence.

Section IV introduces and guides you through the 12 steps in the P2LR and the related core ""Well-Being Competencies" It represents an evidence based, psychodynamic process that is a "true north" shortcut back to happiness. It is a shortcut because it does not require going back in time and turning over all the stones in your life that may have contributed to your unhappiness in the present. Rather, it helps you decide and systematically achieve what you want to be, do, feel, think, own, associate with, and impact by some date in the future. And it does all this in a way that ultimately leads to greater health and happiness.

Section V introduces and explains two "Quick Start" tools that you can use once you have mastered the 12 P2LR steps. These abbreviated routines build on everything that is laid out in the previous sections. They are easy to learn and apply on any pesky problem you want to overcome or goal you want to set and achieve.

SECTION I

FINDING YOUR RECIPE FOR HAPPINESS: STARTING WITH THE END IN MIND

Using the Happiness Algorithm Planner (HAP) to Determine Happiness

In keeping with my earlier quote, "beginning with the end in mind," it is helpful to the process here to clarify that the "end goal" of this book is to increase happiness and serenity. In other words, devoting yourself to the 12 P2LR steps introduced in Section IV will increase your happiness and sense of well-being. This is because it is based on what leading behavioral and social scientists agree are the most important principles and conditions that must be included in any legitimate approach to helping people better themselves, overcome troubles, improve weaknesses, and ultimately lead happier, more serene, and healthier lives.

Another saying that is also relevant here is, "If you do not know where you are going you will have a hard time getting there." This is true with happiness. If you do not know what makes you happy and what you need to think and do to be happy, you may never get there. Moreover, those who do not know their own recipe for happiness are easily mislead by society, science, the different brands of religion, their family and friends, and, above all, marketers who are constantly telling us what we need to think, do, and buy to be happy. As a result, the three essential steps to achieving happiness are 1) understanding what happiness is, 2) identifying your own unique recipe for happiness, and 3) consistently applying the recipe.

The scientific literature continues to grow in consensus around the idea that happiness can be measured in a way that allows us to determine who is happy, what makes them happy, and why (Seligman, 2012; Rath & Hartner, 2010; Graham, 2009; Mcmahon, 2004; Page, Wrye & Cole, 1986). Researchers, including myself (Seligman, 2012; Deiner, 200o; Page & Cole, 1992; Page & Cole, 1991; Cole, 1985) have devised theories, models, and paradigms to help describe happiness and well-being (Fordyce, 2005; Wallace, 2005; Seligman, 2004; Deiner, 2000). Although many of these theories have proven useful, they are relatively inflexible in not accounting for advances in the state-of-the-art research of what happiness is and how to measure it.

In view of the limitations connected with relying on a single theory or paradigm, many researchers and self-help gurus have adopted a trans-theoretical approach to conceptualizing and updating how they think about happiness. That is, rather than relying on one theory, they choose among the most salient factors or features of prominent, well-grounded theories, for a given situation. However, in doing so they can lose the benefits of the structure provided by a theoretical model. Hence, the trade-off for inflexibility is a loss of structure provided by a theoretical paradigm.

In view of this conundrum related to how to define and handle the ever growing knowledge that has been discussed at some length by my co-authors and I in the early 90s (Cole, Holtgrave & Rios, 1993), I am introducing a psychodynamic approach here that has helped me objectively conceptualize and measure the outcomes of therapy and/or self-directed change. The principle advantage of this approach is that it combines the flexibility of a trans-theoretical approach with the structure of a paradigm.

The approach I am introducing here is called the "Happiness Algorithm Planner" (HAP). In recognition of issues I mentioned above and the fact that no definition can be inclusive and acceptable to all, the HAP does not restrict you to one model of describing happiness or well-being in the process of determining the factors most relevant to accomplishing behavior change. Instead, it transforms the reliance on a single researcher's population-based correlates or causal determinants of happiness to an emphasis on the values and perceptions of each individual who uses the model to isolate their own unique recipe for happiness. Furthermore, the HAP helps the user draw upon the stated principles of several models (the trans-theoretical model) in an attempt to be thorough, comprehensive, and up-to-date with contemporary thinking around what constitutes true happiness.

The basic assumptions underlying the HAP model are as follows: 1) happiness is a subjective state that is based on an individual's perception; 2) individuals can reliably and honestly report their perceived state of happiness as well as increases and decreases in their status; 3) with time and the right support, individuals are capable of determining what makes them more or less happy; and 4) thinking and behaving in ways that do not increase happiness is irrational. In view of these assumptions, I define happiness as a psychological state of subjective well-being that results from thinking and living rationally—in a way that is consistent with what a person knows, via use of the HAP, makes him or her happy.

After applying the process for an extended period of time, you will begin to isolate the ingredients to your personal happiness algorithms (your happiness recipe). At that point you can begin to make informed decisions about how to use the P2LR process to increase your happiness.

The good news is that you can isolate what you are thinking or doing to cause the chronic pain and adjust accordingly. In fact, the express purpose of the P2LR process is to help you reassert yourself in rational ways that lead to greater happiness.

I suggest that you try experimenting with the Happiness Algorithm Planner (HAP) as a means of identifying your own unique happiness recipe. The HAP will help you begin the process of isolating what makes you happy and then of establishing a plan to systematically increase your overall happiness. In column 1 list those dimensions of happiness that, based on your experience, make the most sense to you. To assist you with the things you might include in this column, I have provided you a list of factors that prominent researchers believe serve as ingredients of happiness.

As you begin to use the HAP you will note that it is like playing the game "Hot and Cold," where you use feedback from your experience and environment to determine what helps you get warmer (closer to happiness) and what causes you to get cooler (farther from happiness). In keeping with this analogy, an example of "getting cooler" would be evidenced by chronic psychological pain. When you experience depression or anxiety, these painful emotions are telling you that your approach to happiness is somehow deficient. Conversely, if your application of the HAP causes you to experience a discernible increase in happiness, you know that what you are thinking or doing is causing you to get "warmer."

More specifically, complete the HAP, shown here as Table 1 : 1) list the factors that you think contribute to your happiness in column 1. For ideas about what researchers consider to be some of the best predictors of happiness, refer to Table 1 ("Happiness Factors Based on Research Findings of Prominent Happiness and Life Satisfaction Researchers"), and 2) in columns 2-7, answer the questions that relate to each "happiness predictor" you have listed in column 1. For instance, the example illustrated in Table 1 lists "pleasure" as a predictor of happiness. If you agree and list pleasure in column 1, ask yourself, a) What do I need to think more about to increase my pleasure? b) What do I need to think less about to increase my pleasure? c) What do I need to do more of to increase my pleasure? d) What do I need to do less of to increase my pleasure? e) Where do I need to spend more time and with whom to increase my pleasure? f) Where do I need to spend less time and with whom to increase my pleasure? Continue filling out the HAP until you have answered the six questions listed in columns 2-7 for each of your "happiness ingredients" listed in column 1. You will soon notice that the information you derive from this process will give you some concrete ideas that you can apply immediately in your quest toward finding your own tailor-made recipe for happiness.

HAPPINESS ALGORITHM PLANNER

Your Happiness Factors	What do you need to think more about?	What do you need to think less about?	What do you need to do more of?	What do you need to do less of?	Where do you need to spend more time and with who?	Where do you need to spend less time and with who?
Pleasure	Tasty food, a good nap, warm bath, lounging on the beach.					
Engagement	The absorption of an enjoyed, yet challenging activity or event.					
Relationships	Relationships with others that contribute to your sense of well-being.					
Meaning	A perceived quest or belonging to something bigger than yourself.					

Table 1

HAPPINESS ALGORITHM PLANNER

Your Happiness Factors	What do you need to think more about?	What do you need to think less about?	What do you need to do more of?	What do you need to do less of?	Where do you need to spend more time and with who?	Where do you need to spend less time and with who?
Accomplishment	Setting and achieving tangible goals.					
Gratitude	Gratitude, thankfulness, or appreciation is a feeling or attitude in acknowledgment of a benefit one has received or will receive.					
Life Balance	Attending to the dimensions of your well-being and making time for the most important things in life, while not being afraid to let go of less important tasks, projects and people.					
Self Image	Liking and accepting yourself the way you are.					

Table 1

Happiness is not to be achieved at the command of emotional whims. Happiness is not the satisfaction of whatever irrational wishes you might blindly attempt to indulge. Happiness is a state of non-contradictory joy — a joy without penalty or guilt, a joy that does not clash with any of your values and does not work for your own destruction, not the joy of escaping from your mind, but of using your mind's fullest power, not the joy of faking reality, but of achieving values that are real, not the joy of a drunkard, but of a producer. Happiness is possible only to a rational man, the man who desires nothing but rational goals, seeks nothing but rational values and finds his joy in nothing but rational actions.

-Ayn Rand, Atlas Shrugged

HAPPINESS FACTORS BASED ON RESEARCH FINDINGS
of Prominent Happiness and Life Satisfaction Researchers

Researcher	Happiness Ingredients
Michael W. Fordyce, "The 14 Traits of Happy People"	1) Be more active and keep busy; 2) Spend more time socializing; 3) Be productive at meaningful work; 4) Get better-organized and plan things out; 5) Stop worrying; 6) Lower your expectations and aspirations; 7) Develop positive optimistic thinking; 8) Get present-oriented; 9) WOAHP—work on a healthy personality; 10) Develop an outgoing, social personality; 11) Be yourself; 12) Eliminate the negative feelings and problems; 13) Close relationships are #1 source of happiness; and 14) Happy people place a very strong value on happiness.
Martin Seligman, "Flourish: A Visionary New Understanding of Happiness and Well-Being"	1) Pleasure (tasty foods, warm baths, etc.); 2) Engagement (or flow, the absorption of an enjoyed yet challenging activity); 3) Relationships (social ties have turned out to be extremely reliable indicators of happiness); 4) Meaning (a perceived quest or belonging to something bigger); and 5) Accomplishments (having realized tangible goals).
Ed Diener, "Happiness: Unlocking the Mysteries of Psychological Wealth"	1) Psychological wealth is more than money; 2) It is also your attitudes, goals, and engaging activities at work; 3) Happiness not only feels good, but is beneficial to relationships, work, and health; 4) It is helpful to set realistic expectations

Table 2

HAPPINESS FACTORS BASED ON
RESEARCH FINDINGS (continued)
of Prominent Happiness and Life Satisfaction Researchers

Researcher	Happiness Ingredients
Ed Diener, "Happiness: Unlocking the Mysteries of Psychological Wealth"	about happiness; 5) No one is intensely happy all of the time; and 6) Thinking is an important aspect to happiness.
Gallup-Healthways Project	Life balance is important to happiness and includes 1) How you evaluate your life, 2) Physical health, 3) Emotional health, 4) Healthy behavior, 5) Work environment, and 6) Your basic access to develop and prioritize strategies to help your community thrive and grow.
The Seattle Area Happiness Initiative	1) Rational self image; 2) Psychological maturity and well-being; 3) Physical health; 4) Time or work-life balance; 5) Social connection and community vitality; 6) Education; 7) Access to arts, culture, and recreation; 8) Environmental quality and access to nature; 9) Good governance; 10) Material well-being; 11) Meaning; 12) Accomplishments; and 13) Personal and interpersonal character (worth and potential, rights and responsibilities, fairness and justice, care and consideration, effort and excellence, social responsibility, and personal integrity), skills (self-control, delay of gratification, persistence, critical thinking, coping with peer pressure, conflict resolution, prioritizing competing standards, and goal setting).

Table 2

Once again, the end goal of this book is to help you systematically re-engineer or reprogram your beliefs, thoughts, actions, and view of yourself in a way that will help you achieve a state of happiness, regardless of what is going on in your life. This is important given that those who are ignorant of their "happiness recipe" will invariably think and do things that make you unhappy without even knowing it. The purpose of the 12 P2LR steps are to help you create a vision of your highest and best self and to create a plan that will help you realize this vision toward increasing your overall happiness and contentment in life. With time, applying the process—if my claims about the process are true, and they are—will enlarge, deepen, broaden, and amplify your highest aspirations for happiness, health, and a sense of true serenity. It will bring about a fundamental change in your beliefs, heart, and life.

Inner happiness is a quality of spirit which must be earned by a victory over our weaknesses and an upward reach for the perfection of our character. It is like swimming upstream. It is found in the great efforts and achievements of life and in faithful devotion to duty.

-Anonymous

SECTION II

HOW DOES TRUTH RELATE TO RATIONALITY & HAPPINESS?

The process, tools, and techniques I introduce here are based on the concept of rationality. The key criteria used to determine whether or not something is rational is objective truth. That is, if something is not true, it is not rational. With this in mind, I will briefly review my thoughts on both truth and rationality as a means of setting the stage for the ideas and techniques that follow.

I am always humored by the phone calls I get from potential clients asking how much I charge for a session. As I mentioned earlier, I typically ask them if their sole criteria for selecting a therapist is cost. And, in many instances, they say yes. At that point I try to explain to them that selecting a person who will sit and listen to your deepest secrets and, in turn, attempt to help you get better should be based on more than saving a few dollars. Not all therapists, just like not all attorneys, plumbers, and pilots, are the same. There is a great joke that makes my point. "Do you know what they call a medical student who graduates last in his class?" And, the punch line is, "They call a medical student who graduates last in his or her class a doctor!" This analogy is my preface to this section of the book, which is designed to remind you that not all "self-help" or "self-directed change processes" are the same. Most are written by individuals who are effective writers but lack in experience, background, or understanding of behavioral science. And some are simply great storytellers who play on the existential, hedonistic leanings of humans who want to find a shortcut to paradise and greatness. In contrast, this book is a valuable investment because the principles and processes described here are both scientifically (truth) based and clinically proven to be effective.

An essential element that serves as a defining characteristic of a rational self-identity, of rational thinking, and of rational living, is that they are all based on scientific truth, i.e., they are logical and consistent with known facts and reality. With this caveat in mind, I believe it is important to address the growing popularity of moral relativism. Moral relativism is an irrational philosophy that often competes with the bedrock principles that must be applied to bring about effective individual and interpersonal change, growth, and true happiness.

My concern about moral relativism comes from my worldwide experiences that have demonstrated the irrationality of this philosophy that simply does not stand up against natural laws. Rather, it is based on theoretical fun and games comprised of "made-up rules" that simply do not make sense in the real world.

In short, many of the proponents of moral relativism act as if they believe the universe rearranges itself to accommodate their view of reality. This is evidenced by their attempts to either deny or attempt to rewrite natural laws for expediency's sake by simply justifying irrational attitudes and actions that are convenient rather than being based on collective wisdom and science. For example, a true moral relativist would not consider it a problem if a man cheated on his wife as long as his wife did not find out. On the surface and in the moment, this makes some sense. However, when the wife later discovers she has HIV or an STD, the relativists' hedonistic existential argument that "if it feels good do it" breaks down on many levels. Why? Because the irrational idea that one human being can violate the trust of another human being without consequences is based on a lie. The truth is, all actions have consequences and simply justifying an action does not remove the consequences. Put another way, those who practice the philosophy of moral relativism promote the irrational belief that a person can think or do anything he or she wants to think or do without any real predictable consequences. Once again, the truth is, we can think or do what we want to do but, in most cases, we have no control over the consequences that follow the natural laws of our universe.

For many years I worked in the area of HIV prevention,

both in the U.S. and abroad. I was tirelessly trying to persuade individuals and populations about the dangers of certain behaviors. During this time I had a dream, which was no doubt a projection of my frustrations related to my failure to convince many people to change their irrational behaviors. In the dream I saw a large building, and in the building were many people who were randomly running across a room in the center of the building. In the middle of the room was a huge opaque crystal about the same diameter as a large oak tree. Those people who ran directly through the center of the room ran into the crystal. The effects were devastating. When I saw this, I went to the center of the room and started yelling out a warning about the presence of the crystal. In spite of this warning, many individuals continued to run directly into the solid mass, which began to turn red because of the trauma experienced by those who collided with the crystal at top speeds. When I awoke I realized I was simply releasing some pent up frustration in my nightmare. My frustration was with the fact that those individuals I was trying to help were simply dismissing the negative consequences of their irrational actions.

For example, on one assignment to Uganda where I was working on the AIDS problem, I was staying in the only modern hotel in the capital city of Kampala. After spending the day in villages where, in some cases, it was estimated that 1 in 3 adults were infected with the virus that causes AIDS, I would come back to my hotel where men from all over the developed world were picking up female prostitutes who were, by that time, all infected with the virus. These men who were away from their families for extended periods of time were justifying engaging in sexual relations with complete strangers who were giving them more than transitory pleasure. In speaking with some of these individuals it was obvious that they had the irrational belief that they were immune to the consequences of their behavior. What was most disturbing was their callous disregard for how their behaviors could and, in many cases would, impact their loved ones who were ignorant of what was going on in the lives of these men.

I have used the word "consequences" many times in my attempt to explain what I mean by the effects of decisions made on the basis of irrational thoughts and actions. This is because consequences are inevitable in the application of principles that are based on truth. To argue otherwise is to say that there is no truth and no law governing the universe. It is like saying it is ok to put water in your gas tank instead of gas. After all, both water and gasoline are liquids; therefore, it does not make any difference what kind of liquid you put in a fuel tank because all liquids are created equal, right?

Other examples of how ridiculous it is to believe that there are no consequences associated with certain irrational beliefs and behaviors or that "consequences are relative" include the idea that a person can substitute rat poison for flour when baking cookies without causing harm to those who eat them; or that five different people can add the same column of numbers and get different results and that all results are correct; or to say that a person can drive a car from New York to Amsterdam without getting wet; or that it is ok for a dog to drink soda instead of water because it tastes better. My point here is that there are countless examples of natural laws all around us, which suggests that all things in our universe must adhere to these laws.

My experiences as a therapist have shown me over and over again that universal laws also apply to human behavior. As I explained in the Preface, I call them universal because they apply across cultures, time periods, races, and religions. Universal laws link human behavior to certain consequences, providing predictability and a sense of certainty and control over our lives. By understanding respecting these laws, we receive a reassurance that life is not a game of chance, but a rich experience that can lead to a true sense of happiness and fulfillment.

As I explained in the Preface, I spent much time during my youth on a large cattle ranch. There I learned the importance of "reaping what I sowed." I knew that if we planted a garden we had to take certain steps to ensure that we would have a successful harvest. We needed to till the ground, plant good seeds, fertilize, weed, water, and protect our crops from predators. When we respected these laws of the harvest, that is, when we followed universal laws of farming, we always produced something that was edible.

Although this analogy may seem simplistic, it demonstrates how thoughts and behaviors lead to consequences. When we behave rationally, we can expect to reap the benefits of healthy and rational living. And when we behave irrationally, we can expect to reap the pains of irrational living. Unfortunately, sometimes those who have written about psychology and how it applies to individuals and their relationships tend to leave out this link between irrational thoughts, behaviors, and consequences. This is because many of the theories taught in graduate school focus on theoretical "guesses" and often overlook the psychological "common sense" that must be learned through experience.

I saw an example of the inadequacies of graduate clinical psychology training play out in a small rural community during our annual summer parade. While moving slowly down Main Street, one of the small trucks pulling a float suddenly stopped running. Alongside the parade route where this incident happened was the newly hired "county psychologist." Wanting to be helpful, he ran out and helped guide a much larger truck in front of the stalled truck, to back up close enough so the larger truck could tow the smaller truck to the end of the parade route. After the lead truck was in place, the driver handed the new county psychologist a chain that he, in turn, connected to the hitch of the lead truck and then connected to the plastic grill cover of the stalled vehicle. When an elderly farmer witnessed this strategy, he kindly approached the psychologist and suggested that the chain be attached to the frame of the stalled truck instead of the plastic grill. The psychologist was immediately convinced that the farmer knew what he was talking about and reattached the chain to the truck frame.

What was most impressive to me at the time was that this learned doctor was humble enough to admit his mistake and make a change. This was a surprise to me because I was trained by some of the leading academics in my field and I am convinced that they would have dismissed the farmer's advice and made elaborate excuses when the plastic grill of the stalled truck broke under the pressure of the tow. This is not meant to be an attack on anyone. Rather, it is just a reminder that not everything that sounds good or looks good on paper or, that is pontificated over the alters of a major University, is rational or factual. As an academic myself, I must also admit to not always seeing things clearly. After years of working with people, many of the theories of human behavior that I taught my students as a young professor simply do not hold up in a clinical setting.

There are true principles that can be learned and applied in predictable ways that increase the likelihood of individual and interpersonal development and true happiness. In fact, it is the application of these "true principles" and the logic they support that differentiates this book and the change process introduced in Section III, labeled Plan 2 Live Rationally (P2LR), from a more simple-minded approach to self-improvement and change. For example, a blog post or a laymen's article about change will no doubt include information about the importance of goal setting.

This is because it is no secret that change and personal improvement require direction. And, it is also no secret that the best way to chart a specific direction in life is to set a goal. What is a secret to individuals who have never had to earn their pay by helping people change, is that the ability to achieve any goal requires two important elements: 1) believing you are someone who can achieve the goal, and 2) actually being someone who has what it takes to achieve the goal. Both of these conditions are necessary. However, neither of these conditions, independent of the other, is sufficient to achieving a particular goal. To achieve, you must both believe and have what is required to achieve. This is because believing something is true does not make it true. It makes it possible, but not true. Something is true only when it is rational. And something is rational only when it is based on fact. This means if you believe you can do something that you can actually do, your belief is true. On the other hand, if you believe you can do something that you cannot actually do, it is a fact that you believe in something that is not true

Once again, this is to illustrate that simply saying something does not make it true. Universal, objective truth is elusive and can only be discovered through rigorous controlled trials and experiences that consistently demonstrate that some permutation or combination of variables always brings about the same outcome. That said, the P2LR process introduced and described in Section IV is true because if applied as prescribed, it predictably brings about desired changes and increased happiness. In large measure, the reason for this predictability is due to the fact that the process teaches the user how to learn and master techniques that ensure both rational thoughts and behaviors. With this in mind, it is important to understand what I mean by rational thoughts and behaviors.

In the most basic epistemology, rational thoughts and actions should be based on objective truth and logic. However, because not everyone's logic is actually logical, it helps to add some additional criteria when differentiating between rational and irrational thoughts and actions.

Generally speaking, behavioral scientists and cognitive therapists agree on a number of factors that characterize rational thoughts. Most agree that for a thought to be rational it must 1) be logical and consistent with known facts and reality—based on truth; 2) produce desired emotions; 3) help overcome current and future problems; 4) encourage serenity, personal growth, development, and happiness; 5) encourage learning from the past, preparing for the future, and living in the present; 6) support personal and interpersonal goals; and 7) support an optimistic view of one's self and future. Conversely, a thought is irrational if it 1) is not logical and/or there is no evidence to support it as true; 2) does not help you feel the way you want to feel; 3) does not help you overcome your problems; 4) is destructive to yourself or others; and/or 5) undermines your goals.

As is the case with rational thoughts, rational actions can be further clarified with some specific criteria. Accordingly, rational behaviors 1) have a basis in reality to support their intended effects; 2) contribute to health, personal growth, and emotional maturity; 3) increase happiness; 4) help you feel the way you want to feel; 5) help you achieve your goals; and 5) support a Rational Self Perception or RSP. As with irrational thinking, actions that 1) do not help you feel the way you want to feel, 2) do not help you overcome your problems, 3) are destructive to yourself or others, and/or 5) undermine your goals, are considered irrational.

Taken together, rational thoughts and actions translate into what I refer to as rational living. This means that any time you increase your rational thinking or actions, you are increasing your overall rationality. This is important because, based on everything I have observed in my clinics and population interventions and research, there is a direct correlation between increased rationality and happiness. In other words, if you increase your rational living, you will experience increased happiness. Because being happy is more rational than being unhappy, all thoughts and behaviors that increase life satisfaction are labeled "rational." In contrast, thoughts and actions that reduce life satisfaction are classified as "irrational" because they reduce happiness.

The connection between rationality and happiness will be explained and demonstrated in more detail in Section III. However, before going through this explanation and how it relates to the P2LR process, the next section (Section II) will provide you with a deeper level of understanding regarding the principles, assumptions, and logic behind the P2LR process and why the steps laid out in Sections III and IV are both necessary and sufficient for personal and interpersonal change and development.

SECTION III
LOGIC MODELS & PRINCIPLES
FOR CHANGE

Stress Response Cycle (SRC)

I believe the principles and processes described in this book are universally true because they have worked in the past, they work now and, without exception, they will work in the future. This is illustrated in Figure 1, which is the "Stress Response Cycle" (SRC) I use to help my clients understand and apply the self-directed change process required to move forward in their lives. When working with my clients I explain, as is illustrated in this Figure, the following principles:

> 1) all individuals, couples, families, and organizations experience problems that, in turn, cause emotional stress and pain;

> 2) when problem-induced pain is detected and, especially when it becomes intolerable, coping efforts are undertaken to reduce or eliminate the pain;

3) different types of coping (rational versus irrational) can make the original problem better or worse;

4) coping in healthy, rational ways makes people stronger; and

5) whether or not it temporarily reduces stress in the short-term, coping in unhealthy, irrational ways makes people weaker and more dependent.

The SRC provides context and direction in the process of identifying, mitigating, and overcoming problems across both the psychological and behavioral spectrums. I will explain this in detail, beginning with the construct I call "SRC problems."

STRESS RESPONSE CYCLE

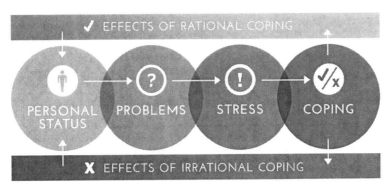

Figure 1

SRC Problems: Practical Versus Psychological

In the context of this SRC, problems are those people, places, and things that we encounter on a daily basis that cause us stress. They come in all sizes, from small to overwhelmingly large.

From a psychological perspective, problems are those things we register in our minds as discrepancies between the way things are and the way we would like them to be. In a broad sense, a problem exists when an individual becomes aware of a significant difference between what actually is and what is desired. For example, if you wake up with pain in your shoulder and you do not want to experience pain (only the true masochist does), you have a problem—you are experiencing pain. If the undesirable pain is great, the discrepancy between your desire to be like most people, pain free, is great. Therefore, you have a big problem, which will cause stress and motivate you to cope.

From a psychotherapist's perspective, psychological discrepancies that people label or perceive to be "problems" are different for each person. That is, what is perceived to be a problem for one individual may be quite different from what is considered problematic to the same person's spouse, friend, child, or the person next door. For example, some people love to get attention in public settings whiles others are terrified. Some people love to exercise while others hate to sweat. Some people desire great wealth while others are satisfied with small means. Some parents expect perfection from their children while others are happy if their children stay out of jail.

SRC: Stress

Humans experience stress from birth. Stress is a normal response to anything that makes us feel keyed up, threatened, or upset (Cole, Tucker & Friedman, 1990; Cole, Tucker & Friedman, 1986; Cole, 1985). Consequently, when a person experiences a problem, they also experience stress. In other words, when people, places, or things are not the way we want them to be, we experience stress.

Stress can be a good thing when it motivates you to escape from a dangerous situation or when it helps you stay energetic and alert. However, when it causes chronic psychological or physical pain, stress is a message to our brain that something is wrong. This message motivates us to think or do something to get rid of the pain.

SRC Coping: Is it Rational?

The things we think and do to get rid of this pain are called Coping Responses. Because stress is a form of pain and, because we are programmed from birth to react to pain, when we experience stress caused by a problem we begin coping in an effort to reduce the pain. For an infant, the typical coping response to pain is to cry out. As we get older, our coping responses become more sophisticated.

And, in every case, the coping responses we engage in are designed to remove the pain. For example, if we have normal sensation in our fingers and we touch a hot stove, we quickly pull back in response to the pain.

Some very important truths about coping are illustrated in the "SRC Coping Window" in Table 3. First, it should be noted that there are two broad types of coping. These can be labeled here as rational and irrational. The terms rational and irrational are interchangeable with terms like healthy and unhealthy, wise and unwise, right(eous) and unright(eous), effective and ineffective.

As can be seen in this diagram, both types of coping are the same, with one exception. Rational coping makes an individual stronger whereas irrational coping makes a person weaker. This is one of the keys to understanding why two similar individuals who have the same problem end up in very different places. For example, the outcomes will be very different for a person who drinks alcohol to deal with stress and another person who engages in aerobic exercise like running and cycling to relieve the stress-induced pain (Page & Cole, 1991; Cole, Tucker & Friedman, 1990). Admittedly, both individuals will get some relief. However, because of the addictive properties of alcohol, the person who relies on this unhealthy means of coping will need increasingly higher doses of this drug to function due to tolerance and may gain weight due to the increased calories. While at the same time, the person who exercises will get the same benefit, stress reduction, as well as weight loss and all the benefits associated with fitness. Another example is a person who screams at his or her spouse to win an argument while another person engages in a reasonable conversation until the argument is resolved peaceably. In both cases there is relief from stress. However, in the case involving reason, the long-term outcome will be more desirable.

SRC COPING WINDOW

Characteristics of Rational, Healthy, Wise, Effective, Right(eous) COPING RESPONSES	Characteristics of Irrational, Unhealthy, Unwise, Ineffective, Unright(eous) COPING RESPONSES
A way of thinking or acting in response to stress	A way of thinking or acting in response to stress
Relieves pain caused by stress	Relieves pain caused by stress
Requires mental or physical effort	Requires mental or physical effort
Requires varying degrees of discipline	Requires minimal if any discipline. Referred to as "the Path of Least Resistance," or the "Softer, Easier Path"
Oftentimes more difficult in the short term	Often easier in the short term and more difficult in the long term. Referred to as a "quick fix"
Requires internal locus of control	Rooted in external locus of control
Helps achieve rational goals	Prevents achievement of rational goals

Table 3

SRC COPING WINDOW CONTINUED

Characteristics of Rational, Healthy, Wise, Effective, Right(eous) COPING RESPONSES	Characteristics of Irrational, Unhealthy, Unwise, Ineffective, Unright(eous) COPING RESPONSES
Is moral, ethical, and legal	In some instances, is immoral, unethical, or illegal
Requires personal resilience that is commensurate with the amount the magnitude of the adversity encountered	Does not require resilience
Makes an individual stronger, healthier, more independent, wiser, more effective	Makes an individual weaker, unhealthy, more dependent, unwise, less effective

Table 3

SRC: Outcomes

Those who prefer "quick fixes" to stress, like drinking to relax, or smoking marijuana to forget, or quitting a job to escape an uncomfortable workplace, or retreating from a stressful situation (such as speaking in public), tend to become emotionally weaker over time. In fact, the worst thing a person can possibly do when he or she has an anxiety disorder is to "retreat from people, places and things" that cause the anxiety. This is because the retreat both relieves the stress caused by the anxiety-provoking situation and, at the same time, reinforces the behavior this person is trying to overcome—the tendency to retreat from things that cause anxiety.

46

Resilience Development Cycle (RDC)

The importance of personal resilience is captured in a quote credited to Ardmore Herophilus who, in 30 BC, was reported to have said, "When Health is absent, Wisdom cannot reveal itself; Art cannot become manifest; Strength cannot be exerted; Wealth is useless and Reason is powerless." As will be discussed in some detail under the "Personal Balance" part of this section, health and personal resilience are essential to happiness and well-being.

Personal resilience has to do with our ability to cope with and bounce back from the stress-inducing problems we encounter on a day-to-day basis. High levels of resilience increase an individual's ability to recover from high levels of adversity and stress. Whereas, low levels of psychological resilience mean a person will have a limited ability to endure and rebound in response to the challenges of life and the distress that follows.

Resilience is not developed in times of great stress. Rather, it is what you rely upon to retain your rationality when you are challenged with any size problem. In other words, it is too late to obtain resilience when you are in the midst of a crisis. Either you will have developed the resilience you need to ride out the crisis, or not. If you do not have it and you face severe challenges, your ability to cope rationally will be severely limited.

Because humans have needs across a number different dimensions (e.g., mental, emotional, physical, social, and spiritual), personal resilience can be impacted by anything that impacts one dimension in either a positive or negative way. In other words, if you exercise on a regular basis (Tucker, Cole & Friedman, 1986), your resilience across all dimensions will, in most cases, be impacted in a positive way. Similarly, if you do not learn the skills or take the time to develop meaningful friendships and social support, your resilience will be impacted negatively given that you will have no one to turn to when you have exhausted all of your personal resources.

The logic model that I use to illustrate how you can build personal resilience is called the Resilience Development Cycle (RDC). The RDC is similar to the SRC in that it illustrates how our personal decisions impact our well-being or, in this case, our personal resilience. The concept illustrated by this model is important to the process of self-directed change because it explains why some people are more tolerant of stress than others. It also illustrates how the choices we make about how we use our discretionary time make us weaker or stronger.

The RDC is provided here as Figure 2. This figure shows that, at its most basic level, human resilience is impacted by how we choose to use our discretionary time.

RESILIENCY DEVELOPMENT CYCLE

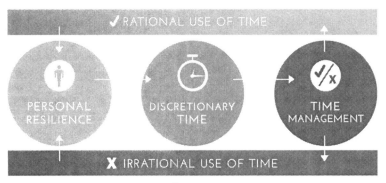

Figure 2

Starting from the left-hand side of Figure 2 and moving to the right, the assumption is that everyone has a finite amount of resilience at any given point in time. The model also assumes that each one of us has a certain amount of discretionary time. And finally, the model assumes correctly that each one of us has the ability to manage our discretionary time in either rational or irrational ways. And, in the case of this model, the rational use of discretionary time means the choice to use this time in a way that makes a person more resilient instead of less resilient. For example, if an unemployed person who wants to get a job but lounges around watching TV most of the day, this behavior would be considered irrational given that watching TV instead of building a good resume, reading the classified section of a newspaper, making phone calls, visiting employment centers and/or exercising to remain fit, is an irrational way of using discretionary time because it does not help the person become more resilient in the area of employment.

Personal resilience is important because it is the energy reserve we have to prepare for life's inevitable difficulties, recover from setbacks, deal with problems, and consciously choose to cope in rational ways in response to any amount of stress induced pain. It is the fuel we need to become better in the face of hardship. The fact is, human beings have known for millennia that if we do not develop resilience and wisely prepare for the future you, we will struggle. This is exemplified in a Proverb in the Old Testament of the Bible as follows (Proverbs 6: 6-11, New American Standard Bible):

> 6 Go to the ant, O sluggard,
>   Observe her ways and be wise,
> 7 Which, having no chief,
>   Officer or ruler,
> 8 Prepares her food in the summer
>   And gathers her provision in the harvest.
> 9 How long will you lie down, O sluggard?
>   When will you arise from your sleep?
> 10 "A little sleep, a little slumber,
>   A little folding of the hands to rest"—
> 11 Your poverty will come in like a vagabond
>   And your need like an armed man.

Building resilience is like the time you put into studying for a test. If it is a very simple test, you do not need to study very much. If it is a big test, you should study a lot and not wait until the last night before the test to start studying.

Just as it takes time to prepare for a big test, it takes time to build resilience. With this in mind, the steps outlined in Section IV provide guidance on how to develop a balanced approach to building and sustaining personal resilience over time.

The "Path of Least Resistance" and "Self-Sabotage": How to Overcome the "Why Not" of Change

I have one more caveat that needs to be explained before introducing the 12-step change process. This has to do with an important principle that is at the heart of the mystery of why people, with the best intentions to make personal changes or to recover from serious addiction, tend to sabotage their best intentions and fail. The key to this mystery is unveiled in a simple diagram in Figure 3, which is an attempt to illustrate the battle between the old and new ways of thinking and doing things—your old self and your new self.

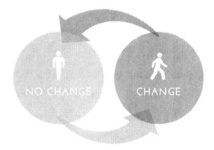

A Tug of War Between Your "Why I should not change" and your "Why I should change"

Figure 3

The fact is, whenever we set out to change we immediately encounter resistance. A simple example of this is in dieting. You may have said to yourself after a big meal that you will never eat that much again. And, in most cases you do not until the next time you are offered a large, tasty meal. A simple explanation of this is that people give in to the pain of hunger because of a lack of self-discipline. Although this is part of the reason, it ignores the real reason. The reason people who vow to quit overeating and fail is because they do not have an important enough goal to carry them past their hunger pains. I call this goal the "Why" of change. This is because whenever we are stressed, we always resort to the "Path of Least Resistance" unless we have a good reason not to.

The "Path of Least Resistance" or the "easier, softer way" is a powerful force that keeps us from growing. It is the reason most people do not set goals, and the reason why most people who do set them do not reach them. It is the reason an abusive person who is contrite after hurting someone goes back to the same behavior the next time he or she is stressed. The fact is, it is easier to do nothing than it is to do something, easier not to try than it is to try, easier to focus on yourself than it is to focus on others, easier to go along with the crowd that it is to adopt a dissenting opinion, easier to settle for a "quick fix" than it is to patiently do what is takes to get the results you want, and easier not to entertain random thoughts than it is to control your thinking. The favorite internal mantra of those who live on this path is simple, "If it feels good, do, and do it until it hurts."

The only way to overcome the gravitational pull of the least resistant path is to set a goal that has a stronger gravitational pull. This is because the strongest pull always wins.

Setting a goal that can overcome the easy path is not that simple. In fact, the recipe for doing this is one of the secret ingredients in the 12-step process outlined in Section IV. What I will say at this point is that it is both necessary and essential to change. Without the "big reason" to change, you simply cannot do it for any length of time.

Behavioral scientists have speculated that part of the reason for the tug of war between easy ways of doing things and ways that require energy and commitment has to do with the part of the brain that is programmed to keep it safe and secure. By definition, this part of the brain (the cerebellum and the brain-stem where reflex responses arise, repetitive routines are stored, and where flight-or-fight attributes are remembered) is more emotional and reflexive than the executive functioning parts of the brain (the cerebrum, frontal lobes, and cortex, where logic, conscious thought, empathy, and art are created) and is considered to be biased against change and stability.

Given that there is a part of our brain that is pulling against change, it makes sense that in order to change, we must somehow overcome the cerebellum's emotional concerns about the unstable condition induced by making life changes. This reflexive part of the brain works against even those life changes that are in our best interest simply because they create a sense of uncertainty. This means that the psychology of change must take into consideration the part of the brain that has concerns about any type of change or instability. To be effective, the process of change must persuade the part of ourselves that is worried about any instability that change is good and in our best interest. The process described in Section IV does just that. And, it does it in a way that convinces the cerebellum and the cerebrum to work together in bringing about the desired change.

Magical Thinking Is Not Magical, or Effective

Another form of self-sabotage is called Magical Thinking. This label should not be confused with "associative thinking," which is a common feature of practitioners of magic. Rather, it is a twisted way of thinking that tends to ignore the steps required to get from point A to Z.

Albert Einstein said, "Genius is 1% talent and 99% percent hard work." I have seen this play out again and again in my clinics where I have tried to help gifted and talented individuals who have successfully made a complete mess out of their lives turn their lives around and get back on a path to sanity.

Most recently, I have experienced a rash of parents making appointments for, and accompanying, their adult "children" to my office for help. The predominant concern is that their "child" is stuck and not making progress. When I hear this I ask the adult child (typically young men, ages 18 to early 30s) if any of his or her parent's concerns are true. In response, the child will often say something like "I just do not have a passion," or "I just do not have any motivation." And, in many cases those who do have passion are unwilling to do anything until they see an opportunity to jump from where they are at in space and time to a place of prominence without taking any steps in between.

One of these young men was 34 years old and was anxiously pursuing a career in Hollywood. He had great passion but was unwilling to go to film school or work for a studio because he perceived that he could "make it big" on his own. This worked for him until one day his parents stopped sending money to help him pay for his car, buy gas, pay rent, and pay for his gym membership. His elderly parents wanted to support his passion, but finally realized their son was engaging in magical thinking.

Although it is been around forever, it seems like magical thinking is becoming more popular than ever before. This may be in some part due to a popular cliché used by some contemporary self-help gurus who promise success to all those who will just "put it out there," whatever that means. Simply put, magical thinking involves thinking and doing things that are believed to have an impact on a specific goal, when in fact the things a person is thinking and doing actually reduce the likelihood of achieving the goal.

In keeping with the above example, the longer the young man puts off going to film school or working his way up the pecking order in the film business, the less likely he is to actually succeed in the business. Even though he "thinks" he is making progress and has made up elaborate stories that he has used to convince his parents and himself that he is making progress, he is actually getting further and further behind as compared to those his age who paid the price of going to film school and working their way up the ranks. Fortunately, and to his parents' great surprise and delight, I was able to work with this young man until he put together a realistic plan that led him to take the necessary steps required to get his career on track.

Frankly, my readers who believe in magical thinking will struggle with what is presented in this book because they will see the process involved as being "too difficult," to which I would ask them, "Why does everything have to be so easy?" Having personally come out of very humble circumstances and risen to a level of success that I never would have imagined as a young man working on a ranch in Southwest, Kansas, I have come to know first-hand the truth of this popular quote by Calvin Coolidge: "Nothing in this world can take the place of persistence. Talent will not; nothing is more common than unsuccessful people with talent. Genius will not; unrewarded genius is almost a proverb. Education will not; the world is full of educated derelicts. Persistence and determination alone are omnipotent. The slogan "press on" has solved and always will solve the problems of the human race." And I might add, magical thinking is often at the core of the belief system of those who think they can succeed without persistence and determination.

Finally, I think the definition of insanity is perhaps the best test as to whether or not you or your loved ones is engaging in magical thinking. That is, "If you keep doing the same thing while expecting a different outcome, you are insane." To get a different outcome you must think and do things differently. You must abandon magical thinking and develop goals and a plan that has been proven to get you where you want to go. This is because you cannot do certain things unless you become the kind of person who does those kinds of things. This means you must study, in great detail, the lives of those who have successfully done the things you want to do, and then you must do those things with a vengeance until you achieve your desired goal.

The fact is, there are no shortcuts to greatness. This was documented in the book, Creativity: Flow and the Psychology of Discovery and Invention, by Mihály Csíkszentmihályi. Based on hundreds of interviews with exceptional people, including business leaders, politicians, biologists and physicists, he found that those who reach great heights in life first master the fundamentals of their chosen profession. That is, none of them engaged in magical thinking, and all of them paid the price of success by carefully cultivating the skills, discipline, and persistence required to excel and make great contributions.

All said, one purpose of this book is to demonstrate what is actually required to achieve and sustain success, happiness, and a sense of well-being. Even if you have incorporated some magical thinking into your personal plans for success and life satisfaction (Who hasn't at some point in their lives?), I recommend that you read this book just to make sure you are not missing something in your personal recipes for living.

The Psychology of Change: Assumptions, Principles, and Conditions Supporting the P2LR

Have you ever wondered why most people who commit to making changes end up giving up on their goals. Part of the secret to this mystery is addressed by the Henry Louis Menken quote that I mentioned in the beginning of this book: "There is always a well-known solution to every human problem—neat, plausible, and wrong." It is true, lasting change and personal improvement is not easy. At the same time, if done correctly, it is not hard. It simply requires following the right steps in the right sequence for the right amount of time. Taken together, the 12 P2LR steps and the corresponding principles, competencies, and skills that support each step will provide you with the essential ingredients required to improve yourself and your relationships. As I have already explained, these ideas are not simply theoretical. Rather, they are based on what leading behavioral and social scientists agree are the most important principles that should be incorporated into an effective self-directed process of change (Seligman, 2012; Fordyce, 2005; Deiner, 2000; Fishbein, Bandura, Triandis, Kaufer & Becker, 1991; Page, Wrye & Cole, 1986; Cole, Friedman & Bagwell, 1986; Page & Cole, 1985; Cole, 1985; Skinner, 1953).

Specifically, those who successfully set and achieve goals that lead to sustained happiness and serenity must do the following:

- view themselves in rational ways. This means they must understand that the way they think about themselves (their perception of self) either increases or diminishes their state of happiness and serenity. For example, perceiving yourself in a way that increases your happiness is a Rational Self-Perception (RSP);

- learn to think rationally—in ways that are congruent with rational goals and a RSP;

- learn to behave rationally—in ways that are consistent with rational goals and a RSP;

- have a rational plan for change—a realistic plan that works;

- have an internal locus of control—a belief that in the case of happiness and emotional well-being, it is not what happens to a person, or a person's circumstances, but what the person decides to think and do about what happens to him or her that counts. Those who think and behave in ways that are consistent with this assumption have an "internal locus of control." Whereas, those who think that they are controlled by what happens to them and/or by their circumstances have an "external locus of control";

• must form a strong positive intention (or make a commitment) to change;

• must understand what can be done to build personal resiliency and cope in healthy, rational ways;

• must have basic skills, including mental imagery and rehearsal, goal setting, resiliency development, coping, cognitive restructuring, critical thinking, self-discipline, delayed gratification, persistence, planning, and problem solving;

• must master monitoring personal status and internal monologues;

• must have the mental discipline to align their thoughts with their goals. This assumes they understand that their conscious mind has a voice. This is evident because as humans we talk to ourselves inside all of the time—we think. It is how we know what we are thinking and feeling. The goal is to talk to ourselves (think) in rational ways. Although it is true that we tend to become what we think about most of the time, successfully achieving a goal requires more than positive thinking. In other words, positive thinking is an additive to rational thinking. On the other hand, negative, self-critical thinking (irrational thinking) erodes confidence and obstructs success. It is irrational to think about yourself in negative, critical ways.

• must believe (have confidence) they can do what is required to change--this is called self-efficacy;

• must understand intrinsic and extrinsic motivation and how they impact goal-oriented thinking and action;

• should have a positive reinforcement for doing what they plan to do;

• should understand how to identify and overcome triggers, barriers, and self-sabotage;

• should believe that the advantages of doing what they plan to do outweigh the disadvantages;

• should perceive that there is more social pressure to do what is recommend than not to do it;

• should believe what they plan to do is consistent with their self-image and does not violate their personal standards;

• should understand that everyone who has a healthy brain can learn to live rationally;

• should understand that rational living increases happiness and serenity—emotional well-being.

They should also understand that the brain's ability to change shape over time (neuroplasticity) allows for changes in the brain that result from conscious changes in thinking. This means we can use our minds to change our brains for the better;

• should understand that setting and striving toward specific goals gives an individual the sense that life has purpose and meaning. Furthermore, achieving goals gives a personal a discernible sense of accomplishment that is often referred to as success—the progressive realization of a worthy ideal. Because setting and achieving goals give an individual a sense of purpose and feelings of success, it is rational to set and achieve goals. Conversely, not setting goals or setting goals that are not achieved is irrational. To be rational, a goal must be specific, measurable, realistic, and stated in terms of a specific time period. In addition, you must believe you can achieve the goal (have self-efficacy or confidence) and actually be able to achieve it, i.e., have the required knowledge, skills, and abilities. This is because 1) it is irrational to assume you can achieve a goal that you do not believe you can achieve, and 2) you must become the kind of person who does the kind of thing you plan to do. We must learn to behave rationally—in ways that are consistent with rational goals and a rational self-image.

Once again, the P2LR steps and the corresponding skills that support each step are based on these assumptions and principles that make up what I refer to as core "Well-Being Competencies." Without these assumptions, this process is just another person's attempt at passing along some "good advice."

SECTION IV
THE P2LR -

12 Steps to Self-Directed Change, Personal Development, & Recovery

As a professional who spends most of my time trying to help others, a constant concern that I share with other helping professionals can be summed up by the quotes I referenced earlier. Albert Einstein, "Make everything as simple as possible, but not simpler." Henry Louis Menken said, "There is always a well-known solution to every human problem—neat, plausible, and wrong." There is a concern that I will provide those I am trying to help with either too much or too little information. With this in mind, I have carefully honed the P2LR process into 12 steps that build upon one another.

1. Monitor your personal status.
2. Define and solve problems.
3. Develop and implement a resiliency plan.
4. Create a Rational Personal Vision Statement.
5. Set rational goals.

6. Determine what will motivate you to change and grow.

7. Identify and anticipate triggers and barriers to change and growth.

8. Create a plan of action.

9. Mentally program and internalize your plan of action.

10. Observe and master your internal monologue.

11. Plan to cope rationally.

12. Evaluate your progress and adjust your plan of action.

Each of these steps represents a set of core "Well-Being Competencies" that I believe, based on my clinical experience, every person must master to reach his or her full potential and become and remain happy and serene (i.e., the ability to be OK when things in life are not OK). In other words, mastering the steps and the corresponding will increase your sense of happiness and serenity by helping you consciously and consistently choose rational over irrational thoughts and behaviors.

The competences you will gain by mastering these steps include the ability to

- routinely discern the state of your personal well-being (mindfulness),
- effectively conceptualize and solve problems,
- build and sustain personal resiliency,
- create and maintain a rational self-image,

- set and reach goals,
- motivate yourself to grow and develop,
- identify and anticipate triggers and barriers to change, including personal growth and development,
- create and implement a plan of action,
- mentally program and internalize your rational self-image, goals, and plan of action,
- consciously observe and master your internal monologue,
- cope rationally, and
- evaluate your progress and adjust your plan of action.

The 12 P2LR Steps and the corresponding competencies are provided in Table 4. In this table, the competencies are expressed in the form of a question to help you determine which area you may need more work on as you change and improve your sense of well-being.

P2LR STEPS	P2LR Well-Being Competency Questions
1) Monitor your personal status.	Do I routinely discern the state of my personal well-being (mindfulness)?
2) Define and solve problems.	Can I effectively conceptualize and solve problems?
3) Develop and implement a resiliency plan.	Do I consistently do things to build my personal resiliency routine?

Table 4

P2LR STEPS (continued)	P2LR Well-Being Competency Questions
4) Create a Rational Personal Vision Statement.	Do I have a rational self-image?
5) Set rational goals.	Do I know how to effectively set and reach goals?
6) Determine what will motivate you to change and grow.	Do I know how to motivate myself to change and improve?
7) Identify and anticipate triggers and barriers to change and growth.	Can I identify and anticipate triggers and barriers to change, including personal growth and development?
8) Create a plan of action.	Do I know how to develop and implement a personal progress plan of action? Do you have a plan of action?
9) Mentally program and internalize your plan of action.	Do I know how to mentally program and internalize my rational self-image, goals, and plan of action?
10) Observe and master your internal monologue.	Do I consciously observe and discipline my internal monologue?
11) Plan to cope rationally.	Do I cope rationally?
12) Evaluate your progress and adjust your plan of action.	Can I evaluate my progress and adjust my plans in a way that improves my performance?

Table 4

As you move through the P2LR process you will notice that each step will help you master these competencies by explaining and diagrammatically illustrating the principles that support the competency and by also providing you with specific guidance on how to implement the step. The implementation guidance also includes a number of tools you can use practice to master the step and corresponding competency.

Another way of explaining the P2LR process is in terms of five "Big Ideas." These ideas are illustrated here in Figure 4:

P2LR STEPS	P2LR Well-Being Competency Questions
A	To know how you are doing and whether or not you are making progress, you must monitor how you are doing (P2LR Steps 1, 10 & 12)
B	You can change your life and your future by creating a new persona—becoming a new character (P2LR Step 4)
C	To change your persona (character), you must become motivated to write a new script (goals and a plan of action) that describes how you will think and act in your new role (P2LR Steps 5-8)
D	You must rehearse the script until you take on the new persona and become the new character (P2LR Step 9), and
E	You must think and do what is required to continue playing the new role outlined in your new script and represented by your new persona (P2LR Steps 10-12).

Figure 4

To simplify my explanation, I often use an analogy that occurred to me when I was consulting in Hollywood. I was in Raleigh Studios in Hollywood, CA, talking to several writers and an executive producer of a popular television show. As I was talking about a female character, I had an epiphany that has, from that time forward, improved my ability to help people understand how to apply the therapeutic principles that undergird the psychology of change. As I was talking and the writers were changing the script, I realized the same thing often happens when I am working with my clients. They listen and think through my suggestions, and based on their insights they will "change their script." In fact, I now tell my clients that one of the primary objectives of therapy is to edit their life scripts until they represent the way they want their lives and their futures to play out. With this in mind, P2LR Steps 4-8 are designed to help you write a new script, Step 8 provides you with several powerful tools that help you rehearse and internalize (transport yourself into believing) the script, and Steps 10 and 11 teach you how to function like a television producer who insists on consistency between the script and your acting. The actions taken in Step 12 are like reviewing the ratings that are used to determine whether or not the audience is being impressed.

To take this analogy a step further, the P2LR process is designed to help you, the producer of your life, write a script, rehearse it until it is believable, and then play the part. As my wife once said to me as I was explaining this analogy, "I think you are saying this means that every person is the writer and producer of their own lives, and to get different results you need to change the script—put the information together differently."

This discovery and my ongoing work in Hollywood has continued to remind me of how important it is to understand that each one of us can manufacture a life that is exciting and fulfilling simply by following the steps described here. Truly devoting yourself to this process will cause you to soon be able to discern both fundamental and permanent change in your very nature. This change is made possible through learning to see yourself and your future in a way that allows you to do what is required to become the kind of person who can do the kinds of things you want to do in life. This is because once you create and embrace an image of yourself (your new persona) that is based on your highest and best self, you will naturally conform to this image and reject anything that is incongruent with this new way of being.

In short, every step in the P2LR process is designed to help you systematically re-engineer or reprogram your beliefs, thoughts, actions, and how you view yourself in a way that will enlarge, deepen, broaden, and amplify your highest aspirations for happiness, health, and serenity. It will bring about a fundamental change in your beliefs, heart, and life.

Finally, if for some reason this recipe for change does not work for you, please consider following the advice given in a past television commercial that promoted psychiatric services in the Southwest United States, "If you don't get help here, get it somewhere else." This is because if you do not follow some program or process that leads to more rational living, you will be like the lead character in Groundhog Day. In this movie, a weatherman (played by Bill Murray) finds himself living the same day over and over again until he gets it right. As mentioned before, the best definition of insanity is "thinking and doing the same thing over and over again, expecting a different outcome."

With that said, I will end this introduction to P2LR by repeating one of my favorite quotes by Robert Louis Stevenson: "No man can run away from weakness. He must either fight it out or perish. And if that be so . . . why not now, and where you stand."

One final caveat before you review the steps is the fact that the tables and space provided throughout the book should be considered as guides for recording your ideas. Although there is some space to document your thinking here, I suggest in P2LR Step 1 that you purchase a journal and simply use the tables and spaces for writing provided here as examples that you can transfer to your journal and, in turn, tailor to your own liking and needs. Although any journal will work, you can purchase the P2LR Journal online. The P2LR Journal lists some of the principles included in the book and is laid out to correspond with the order of the P2LR steps.

P2LR STEP 1
Monitor Your Personal Status

Step 1 will help you better understand the value of keeping a daily record in the form of a journal, diary, log, or notebook. Journaling or keeping letters or diaries is an ancient tradition, one that dates back to the beginning of recorded history. This is evident in an ancient Chinese proverb, which says, "The palest ink is better than the sharpest memory." This proverb reminds us that we are more likely to accurately remember things we think and do, or plan to do, when we write them down.

In recent history, journaling has been found to result in both physical and psychological health benefits in both non-clinical and clinical populations. Because of this finding, when I begin working with a new client I often explain that one of the easiest, least expensive, and most profound forms of therapy available is journaling. I explain that fully understanding any experience requires perspective that can be derived from reading your personal history over a period of days and months rather than hours or moments in time. A life recorded page-by-page, day-by-day, month-by-month, and year-by-year reveals patterns, purposes, and relationships between what we think and do and what happens to us over time. When patterns do emerge, you can see more clearly the negative effects of irrational living as well as the benefits of rational thoughts and actions in a way that may have escaped you in the throng of circumstances.

Over the years my clients have used journaling as a tool for self-knowledge, self-insight, self-exploration, self-expression, self-evaluation, and self-improvement. When I have asked them to report back to me the benefits of journaling, I have received many different answers. For example, different clients have told me (I am paraphrasing) that journaling has helped them cope with traumatic experiences; entertain themselves; reframe their negative into more positive experiences; achieve new perspective; ease a sense of loneliness; observe and clarify thinking; improve intuition and creativity; validate the benefits of taking certain actions; process their innermost thoughts; prevent them from making the same mistake twice; become better organized; relive joyful events; increase gratitude for things that have gone right; remind them of what it takes to come back after defeat; remain or become more focused; communicate with themselves; record their deepest concerns and thoughts, achievements, and failures; process events; "organize" their thoughts and feelings; get to know themselves better; realize and release the intensity of their anger, sadness, and other painful emotions; improve congruency between goals, thoughts, actions, and their self-image; stay in the present; track patterns, trends, improvement, and growth over time; ask themselves and answer important questions; record and remember important events; brainstorm solutions to seemingly unsolvable problems and solve their problems more effectively; write about and eventually resolve disagreements with others instead of ruminating over them;

record goals and promises to themselves; capture life story for posterity; hold themselves accountable; evaluate their progress and restore a sense of optimism, anticipation, and excitement about their goals or aspirations.

Although there are many documented benefits to journaling, the primary reason for using this technique in this step is to train you to be more observant. By definition, to be rational you must be observant of what you are thinking and doing. You must also observe how your thoughts and behaviors contribute to, or take away from, your goals and your sense of well-being. In short, developing a habit of journaling will help you develop the habit of being observant in ways that help you extract the lessons from your experiences. For example, instead of focusing on the negative aspect of your experiences you can pay attention to the good that comes out of things that may initially appear to be very negative.

Observing your status will help you record new insights and lessons you learn as you try new ways of thinking and living. As you review this information over time, you will gain the insights you need to break the pattern of doing the same thing and expecting a different outcome. Armed with these insights you can do what is necessary to avoid repeating the same mistakes.

Journaling will help you see your progress over time, which can motivate you to keep moving forward during difficult times. As you look back you will also notice that, in many instances, things you thought were big problems in the past might seem small today. This type of information can also serve as a "reality check" that can remind you that a vast majority of what humans worry about never happen. Mark Twain once so keenly observed, "My life has been filled with calamities, some of which actually happened." This is consistent with a study conducted by professors at the University of Cincinnati who found that eight-five percent (yes - 85%) of what we worry about never happens. The study also reported that 79% of us handle the 15% that does happen in ways that surprise us with our ability to turn the situation around.

To journal, you do not need anything more complicated than a pen and paper or a hardbound journal. I personally prefer a computer so that I can include photos, images, and audio and video clips to enhance my experience both in the here and now and for future reference.

The sooner you record your status, the better. This will prevent you from forgetting exactly what happened.

Finally, to get the most out of journaling it helps to have a plan for what you want to write about. To help you get started I suggest you complete the following assignment. This assignment will help you delve into journaling with a purpose that supports the remainder of the P2LR steps.

Ideas for Implementing This Step & Mastering This Competency

Knowing how you are doing throughout the day is the first step in the process of intentional change. It allows you to determine such things as whether or not you are making progress, what is working and what is not working, beginning to see what is going on inside and outside yourself when you are OK and, when you are not OK.

To begin this personal observation process 1) decide on how you will record your status (e.g., journal, diary, notebook, computer); 2) check your status three times per day and record your answers to the three questions on the "Life Satisfaction Scale;" 3) every night before you go to sleep, write down three things that went well during the day and why; and 4) use the "Hassle Tracker" to identify what is upsetting you on a consistent basis. Perform each of these status checks for at least seven consecutive days.

LIFE SATISFACTION SCALE

(Terrible) 0 -- 1 -- 2 -- 3 -- 4 -- 5 -- 6 -- 7 -- 8 -- 9 -- 10 (Ideal)

Where am I on the scale?
Why aren't I lower on the scale?
What will it take for me to get higher on the scale?

THE HASSLE TRACKER

Use this guide or your journal to begin documenting all the people, places and things you encounter in your day-to-day life that consistently make you upset. In Column 2, write down those things you typically think, feel and do in response to those things that are upsetting you. As you do this exercise, try to identify what things consistently make you upset.

Write down the people, places, and things that cause me to be upset. Record approximately when these things happen to me (Day/Time).	Record what I was thinking, feeling and doing as a consequence of the upsetting things I list in Column 1.

Table 5

MY PLAN FOR P2LR STEP 1

How will I keep track of how I am doing relative to what I am trying to change or improve?

P2LR STEP 2
Define and Solve Problems

Life is difficult! After 38 years of marriage and raising children, I understand this firsthand. Life is also difficult in the workplace. Having worked as a clinician and at the highest levels of local and national organizations, I have encountered problems that I never imagined when I received my doctorate degree and entered the workforce in 1982. Frankly, I have "been there and done that" when it comes to solving many difficult individual and interpersonal problems. Through all of this and more, I have evolved from someone who once avoided problems to a person who sees problems as ripe opportunities for personal and interpersonal growth and development. In fact, as a psychotherapist and public health professional, I make my living solving problems.

This is not to say I enjoy problems. It is, however, to say that learning to rationally conceptualize and solve problems can bring about a great deal of personal satisfaction.

Through all my personal and professional experience, I have learned some important lessons and principles about facing and solving problems that I have incorporated into Step 2 of the P2LR process. Perhaps the most important lesson I have learned is that those individuals who become good at solving problems are highly valued by society, and they experience a greater sense of well-being. This is because they understand some universal truths about the nature of problems, including 1) all people have problems; 2) life is not fair and many problems we experience are caused by circumstances outside our control; 3) problems present opportunities for learning and development; 4) complaining or getting angry is not an effective way of solving problems; 5) being patient and innovative helps when problems are not readily resolved; and 6) learning to effectively solve problems reduces the stress that accompany them.

I once heard a story that has helped me remain patient when dealing with difficult problems. And, given the nature of the work I do, it is not unusual to be challenged on a frequent basis with difficult problems that can, at first, seem overwhelming.

After working on a project in China for a period of time, I decided to hire a driver to take me to visit the Great Wall. On the way to the Wall my driver suggested I stop in a small village and witness the making of different types of pottery. While looking over the pottery I remarked that I loved one of the vases that had the images of running horses painted on the outside. When the guide learned that I was born in the "Year of the Horse," he told me a story that convinced me that I should purchase the vase as a reminder of the principle taught in the story.

Although the story may not be true, my guide told it as if it were, and I am including it here because it illustrates my point. She said that in her village there lived a Zen master who loved horses. One day as he was meditating in the woods near the village, he saw a horse grazing nearby. The master, knowing something about horses, was able to catch the animal and bring it back to the village. When he arrived at the village and corralled the horse, many villagers stopped by the master's house and remarked, "Master, you are very lucky, you captured a horse." In response the master said, "I will wait and see."

The next day the master's newly captured horse broke free and was lost again in the woods. When villagers found out, they stopped by the master's house and said, "Master, you are very unlucky, your horse has escaped." Again, the master said, "I will wait and see." The next day the master's son went out into the woods in search of the lost horse. After searching for a while he found the horse grazing in a meadow. The master's son was able to catch the horse and return it to his father, who then put the horse in a more secure corral. When the villagers heard the news they gathered at the master's home and said, "You are very lucky that your son was able to recapture the horse." As usual, the Zen master said, "I will wait and see."

The next day, the master's son was bucked off the horse when he tried to ride it. When he hit the ground, he broke his leg. When the villagers heard what happened, many visited the master's home and said he was unlucky because his son's leg was now broken. As always, the wise Zen master said, "I will wait and see."

The next day, a group of Chinese soldiers came to the village recruiting young men the age of the master's son to go to a serious battle across the Great Wall against the Mongolian army. That evening, after the dust settled, some villagers stopped by the master's house and said, "You are very lucky because your son broke his leg and did not have to go fight in the terrible battle." And as always, the master responded, "I will wait and see."

I have heard similar stories in many different countries. It is the story of "letting go" or embracing instead of fighting against the things that happen to us as a part of living. The Zen master understood this concept very well. He knew that declaring a problem as lucky or unlucky was unwise because he also understood that we, as humans, do not have control over what happens in our day-to-day lives. Instead of fighting the realities of life, the master simply accepted the events of each day.

In spite of your best efforts, you will have problems. And fighting against, instead of learning to be patient and adapt to, these realities only brings us frustration. Embracing them, even when the events are very painful, allows us to feel peace in the midst of our sometimes-chaotic lives. This is especially relevant when trying to understand and solve difficult problems.

Another important truth about problems is reflected in a quote by Emerson: "For every thousand people hacking at the branches, there is one chopping at the roots." This quote reminds me that before I can solve a problem, I must understand the nature of the problem and what is causing it, i.e., the root cause. Without an understanding of what the problem is and what is causing it, efforts to resolve the issue are oftentimes misguided and ineffective.

There are many good approaches to problem solving. However, the approach I recommend is called the "Problem Solving Planner" or PSP.

Ideas for Implementing This Step & Mastering This Competency

This step provides you with two different approaches to problem solving. The first approach requires that you make a list of the problems you are currently struggling with and then ask yourself a number of questions that are designed to help you think strategically about the problem, its causes, and what you need to think and do differently to address the root causes and overcome the problem.

The second approach uses what is called the "Problem Solving Planner" (PSP). This tool will guide you through a step-by-step process that helps you understand the nature and determinants of the problem before you develop a plan to address it.

1. List the most difficult problems you are currently struggling with. Problems are discrepancies between the way things are in your life and the way you want them to be.

Problem 1:

Problem 2:

Problem 3:

2. How do you feel when you experience a problem?: embarrassed, guilty, angry, sad, incompetent, afraid, anxious, hopeless, unhappy, disappointed, pessimistic, frustrated, regretful, lonely, inferior, panicky, worthless.

    Problem 1:

    Problem 2:

    Problem 3:

3. What do you think or do that contributes to each problem and the negative feelings? This behavior will help you isolate those things you have control over.

    Problem 1:

    Problem 2:

    Problem 3:

4. What can you think or do differently that will help you solve the problem and eliminate the negative emotions? How will these thoughts and actions help you 1) achieve your goals, and 2) feel the way you want to feel? These thoughts and actions should fit the valid thought system in Table 6.

    Problem 1:

    Problem 2:

    Problem 3:

5. What will you do, how often, for how long? What support/resources will you need?

     Problem 1:

     Problem 2:

     Problem 3:

6. Document what you did and did not do, and how you feel as a consequence.

     Problem 1:

     Problem 2:

     Problem 3:

* Assess the rationality of your thinking by asking yourself whether or not the above thoughts and actions have been demonstrated to be effective in helping others solve the kind of problems you are trying to overcome.

As was mentioned above, the second approach you can use to implement this step relies on a problem-solving tool called the PSP. This tool has two phases.

Phase I of the PSP directs you to 1) identify the problem, 2) define it, 3) investigate to determine the causes and possible solutions, 4) decide which causes you will address and which action steps you will take to alleviate these causes, and 5) establish a schedule for monitoring progress and getting feedback that can be used to improve the strategy. In Phase II, you put the information together to make up your intervention strategy, or Problem Resolution Plan.

PSP PHASE I:
Understanding the Problem

Step 1: Identify the Problem	A problem is a "gap" between what "should be" happening and what is actually happening.
Step 2: Define the Problem	Clearly stating the problem you plan to work on is essential to focus on what it is that you plan to change.
Step 3: Investigate to Determine the Causes and Possible Solutions	If you can determine what is causing the problem, then you will be able to focus your attention on the causes rather than the symptoms.
Step 4: Decide Which Causes to Address and Which Steps to Take to Alleviate Them	Once you know what the problem is, and what is causing it, you will be able to select the appropriate action steps to address each cause.
Step 5: Establish a Schedule for Monitoring Progress and Getting Feedback	You must follow up to ensure that each action step is executed.

Table 6

As indicated above, in Phase II of the PSP you put your strategy together. The matrix that follows will help you do this in a systematic way. In column 1, you list what you perceive to be the causes of the problem. In column 2, you describe the action steps you will take in connection with each cause. Finally, in column 3 you record information about when the action steps will be completed.

PSP PHASE II:
Problem Resolution Plan

Cause to Be Addressed	Action Steps	When Actions Are Completed

Table 7

MY PLAN FOR P2LR STEP 2

How will I solve the problems I encounter when trying to change?

P2LR STEP 3
Develop and Implement a Resiliency Plan

Step 3 will help you understand the term resilience and also lead you in creating a plan to manage the stress and challenges in your life. Psychological resilience is an individual's capacity to cope with difficult life events and stress. High levels of resilience increase an individual's ability to cope with and bounce back from high levels of adversity and stress. In contrast, low levels of psychological resilience means an individual will have a limited ability to endure and rebound in response to the challenges of life and the distress that follows.

Resilience is not developed in times of great stress. Rather, it is what we rely upon to retain our rationality when we are challenged with any size problem. In other words, it is too late to obtain resilience when you are in the midst of a crisis. Either you will have developed the resilience you need to ride out the crisis, or not. If you do not have it and you face severe challenges, your ability to cope rationally will be severely limited.

A wise person once said, "By small and simple things, great things (for good or bad) come to pass." For example, to improve my vocabulary I once decided that every day for one year I would learn a new word and how to use it. This allowed me to learn and apply 365 new words. Another good example concerns one of my patients who was bemoaning the fact that, after 22 years of marriage, he was 45 pounds overweight. If you think about it, this individual only put on 2 pounds the first year, and 4 total pounds by the end of his second year of marriage. I am sure he and his wife barely noticed the 4 pounds. However, because he continued at an average increase of weight of 2 pounds per year, he was now sitting in my office 45 pounds overweight. Obviously, had he come to me at the end of the first year, getting back down to weight would have been a reasonably simple task. At least much easier than losing the 45 pounds which, by the way, he did accomplish using this system described here.

My clinical work has consistently demonstrated that those who have the most resilience tend to be individuals who work to keep balance in their lives. Conversely, those who do not put in the time to balance their lives tend to be more reactionary and less likely to respond rationally in the face of life's inevitable challenges. With this in mind, I challenge my clients who are feeling out of control to develop a plan to bring some balance back into their lives. That is, I encourage them to become proactive instead of reactive. To make my point, I often tell them a story about a TV ad that I saw many years ago. The ad, which was designed to sell oil filters, featured a mechanic who made the point that it is better to change your oil and use a good filter than experience major engine problems. This was illustrated by the mechanic when he held up the oil filter and said "pay me now" (for the filter) or "pay me later" (for major engine repair) at which time he pointed to a car on a lift in his garage.

I believe the same principle applies to people. That is, if we do not practice prevention, we will pay a bigger price down the road. Further, because we are multi-dimensional, I believe it is important that we pay attention to all dimensions of ourselves to ensure good health and well-being.

As much as anything, this idea has to do with living a balanced life. By practicing prevention across the different dimensions of your being (physical, mental, social, emotional, and spiritual dimensions), you will attain balance which will, in turn, reduce major problems down the road.

Figure 5 shows some of the dimensions of resilience and personal balance across the Stress Response Cycle (SRC) continuum. A brief description of each dimension, along with some specific examples of why it is important to proactively build and maintain balance across each dimension of resilience, is provided below.

RESILIENCE VARIABLES ACROSS THE SRC

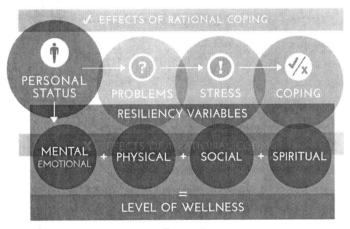

Figure 5

Physical Dimension:

The effects of not consistently paying attention to this dimension are oftentimes more obvious than the other dimensions. For example, if a young adult who is at their ideal weight at age 20 puts on 2 pounds per year for 40 years, they will be 80 pounds overweight by the time they reach 60. Whereas the first year the 2 additional pounds do not seem like much at all, the consistent increase amounts to a lot. Along the same lines, if we do not apply self-restraint on a regular basis in terms of how much we eat, we can put on excess pounds, and most adults know, by sad experience, the price they must pay to overcome unwanted body weight.

It is important to our physical dimension that we exercise on a regular basis. For instance, exercise physiologists have determined that if we exercise aerobically (walk, jog, skate, bike, etc.) most days each week, for at least 20 minutes per session, we will experience a positive "training effect" on our heart, lungs, and blood vessels. The subsequent benefit of such a training effect can also serve to illustrate the interrelationship between the dimensions of our well-being spoken of earlier. That is, in addition to receiving physical benefits such as reduced heart disease, lower percent body fat, lower blood pressure, lower blood cholesterol, and so on, those who engage in aerobic exercise on a regular basis also receive mental health benefits such as improved self-esteem, enhanced perception of body image, decreased depression and anxiety, as well as social benefits such as a fuller social life because of an enhanced appearance and an improved attitude and zest for living. In fact, researchers in California (Belloc & Breslow, 1972) who studied the lives of 7,000 men and women found a relationship between physical well-being and years of life lived to adherence to seven basic practices: sleeping seven to eight hours each night, eating three meals a day at regular times with little snacking, eating breakfast every day, maintaining desirable body weight, avoiding excessive alcohol consumption, getting regular exercise, and not smoking. This report also indicated that men at age 45 who follow three or fewer of these practices, can expect to live to 67; however, men in the same age group who follow six to seven of these practices could expect to live to 78. Similarly, women at age 45, who follow three or fewer of these practices, can expect to die at 74, while women who abide by six or seven of these practices can expect to live to 81.

A more recent example of how being proactive about our health can produce benefits is revealed in a study released by a Scientific Committee in the United States in 2012. This committee reported that up to 50% of cancer in men and women could be prevented by taking a number of proactive steps, including 1) reducing tobacco consumption; 2) increasing physical activity; 3) improving nutrition habits; 4) increasing evidence-based screening and early detection; 5) increasing proven cancer-preventive vaccinations; and 6) increasing protection against excessive UV light exposure of tobacco.

Mental and Emotional Dimension:

The "pay me now or pay me later" concept can also be applied to mental health. Given that how you see yourself (self-esteem or self-image) is one of the best indicators of mental health, any threat to your perceived self-image is a threat to your emotional well-being and happiness. Furthermore, given that self-image is essentially the outcome of a succession of failures and successes in thinking rationally, each time you choose to think rationally about yourself, your image of self improves. This means that a person who is suffering from negative self-image can take proactive steps to improve his or her self-image by thinking and doing things that improve their self-estimation.

Another threat to a rational image that illustrates how the "pay me now or later" construct applies to the emotional dimension of our resilience has to do with the interrelationship between our values and our personal behavior. For example, it is has been demonstrated that individuals who consistently behave in a manner that deviates from their core values experience a more negative perception of themselves—a less rational self-image. With this in mind, I encourage my clients to clarify their personal values and take steps to ensure that their thoughts and behaviors are consistent with their core beliefs and values.

Intellectual Dimension:

Development or lack of development of your intellect also plays a role in happiness and well-being. If you do not "pay now" by consistently studying and assimilating new and diverse information—particularly in our highly specialized and technological society—you will likely pay the price later of under- or un-employment, and need major retraining. This is all to say that because we live in an information age when the proliferation of information is occurring at an unprecedented rate, one of the most important personal resiliency activities you can engage in on a regular basis is self-directed learning.

Social Dimension:

Without a doubt, our social development or adeptness is key to health and well-being. If you do not "pay the price" to learn and practice good social skills, you may struggle in your relationships with family members, peers, and employers. The costs associated with not acquiring these skills can include poor relationships, the inability to make and keep friends, marital problems, and being passed over for desirable jobs or promotions. This dimension is of particular concern in modern society where effective face-to-face communication is rapidly being replaced by social technologies, and where the virtual worlds of video gaming are being substituted for "real world" activities required to develop the social competence required to function effectively in one's personal and work life.

Spiritual Dimension:

Considerable research in recent years has documented what the prophets and wise men have passed down through the ages, which is, attention or lack of attention to our spiritual and character development dimension can and does have a measurable impact on health and happiness. If you do not meet your needs in this area by and through such things as serving others, meditation and prayer, reading inspirational literature, learning the difference between good and bad/right and wrong, and other things that have been documented to improve spiritual health and character development, you can become seriously spiritually malnourished and be unprepared when confronted with the life crises that we all encounter.

Multi-Dimensional Considerations:

Taken together, the dimensions I have just described, if addressed appropriately on a consistent basis, can increase your personal resilience and, in turn, increase the likelihood that you will be happy, healthy and effective in all that you do. It should be noted, however, that to attain and maintain balance, the pursuit of meeting these needs should always be looked at as a means to an end rather than an end in itself. Many people, who get stuck on being popular or attaining big muscles or lots of money at the expense of developing all areas, lose perspective and become imbalanced in their approach to living. Although it is not a bad thing to focus attention on one area or another, balance across all of these dimensions should be considered the ideal means toward the end of becoming a healthy, happy individual, who has the drive and resiliency necessary to realize a vision of the highest and best self-image.

Ideas for Implementing This Step & Mastering This Competency

A simple way to incorporate resiliency into your daily life is illustrated in Table 8. Because small and simple steps over time can lead to great accomplishments, using this type of a guide to set in place activities that you will do on a regularly scheduled basis to improve your resilience will, in turn, ensure that you are getting stronger and not weaker in each of the dimensions described above.

MY DAILY RESILIENCY ROUTINE

Specifically, what will I do on a daily basis to strengthen myself, when will I do it, where will I do it, and for how long will I do it?							
	Mon	Tues	Wed	Thur	Fri	Sat	Sun
Physically							
Intellectually							
Socially							
Spiritually							
Mentally & Emotionally							

Table 8

ADDING A RESILIENCY PLAN TO THE STRESS RESPONSE CYCLE

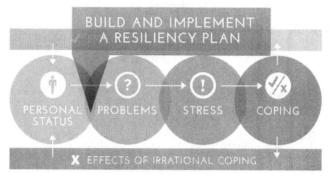

Figure 6

Complete and begin implementing the "Resiliency Plan Matrix." This will help you clarify your personal goals, anticipate your problems, prepare to cope in rational ways, and increase your stress tolerance.

RESILIENCY PLAN MATRIX
(Review This Plan Before You Start Your Day)

1. Here are my most important short- and long-term goals. I will review these daily.

2. Throughout the day, I will ask myself the following questions to determine whether or not my thoughts and actions are rational. Answering no to any of these questions indicates I am thinking or behaving irrationally.
- Does the thought or action motivate me?
- Does the thought or action encourage personal growth, emotional maturity, independence of thinking and action, and mental stability?
- Does the thought or action help me feel good?
- Does the thought or action help me achieve your goals?
- Is the thought based on fact?
- Has the thought or action been proven to help me achieve success?

RESILIENCY PLAN MATRIX (continued)
(Review This Plan Before You Start Your Day)

4. Here are the problems that typically give me difficulty or that I anticipate will cause the most stress during my day/week/month.	
5. Specifically, what will I think today that will help me overcome the items I listed in row 4 above?	
6. Specifically, what will I do today to overcome the things I listed in row 4 above?	
7. Where can I spend time today and/or with whom can I spend time that will help me avoid temptation and achieve my goals?	

Table 8

Obviously, you can use any number of formats for laying out a daily resiliency or "daily good habit" plan. There are also many tools, including SmartPhone Apps, that can help you remember your plan and document your progress. One example of a simple, yet powerful plan is provided below.

Daily Habits for Success and Increased Happiness

1. Do the things I have listed on my resiliency plan (this assumes I have a resiliency plan).

2. Set and achieve at least one new small, measurable goal each day.

3. At the end of the day, ask myself, "What went well, and what went poorly today?" For each thing that did not go well, decide what I can think and do differently to increase the likelihood that this will not happen again. If I have no control over the situation, decide what I can think that will help me feel better about it.

4. Practice being grateful for my problems. When I experience a problem think to myself, "I am grateful for the problems I experienced today because, even though they are difficult and painful, each one of them presents an opportunity for personal growth and development." After all, this statement is true. When I experience and rationally cope with problems, I become stronger. A good example of this is weight lifting. When I lift weights, the muscles being taxed send a message to my brain that causes the flexed muscles to overcompensate and grow.

5. Each time I experience a problem or difficult life event, I will think or do the following things, INSTEAD OF thinking or doing things that have upset me in the past:

6. Before going to bed, I will think of three things I can be grateful for and why.

Table 9

MY PLAN FOR P2LR STEP 3

What will I do to build and maintain my resilience?

P2LR STEP 4
Create a Rational Personal Vision Statement

The quote I referenced in the Introduction by Patrick Rothfuss has direct application to this step. He said, "It's like everyone tells a story about themselves inside their own head. Always. All the time. That story makes you what you are. We build ourselves out of that story."

This quote reminds me that what we believe and think about ourselves and our future matters. It is so important that no matter how hard we try to change, we cannot make significant progress until we begin to see ourselves in ways that are congruent with what we are trying to accomplish. Because of this, before you start changing you must make adjustments to the way you see yourself. If you do not, your subconscious will work against (resist) any goals that are not congruent with your self-perception.

Step 4 will help you create a Rational Personal Vision Statement or RPVS. When completed, your RPVS will represent a rational (based on objective truth), optimistic, broad-based, mental model of your highest and best self and of a bright and promising future.

As you will notice, as I explain the purpose and actions required to complete this step, I will consistently use words like "see" and "visualize." This is because this step and the steps that follow include a number of activities that tap into the right side of your brain, the hemisphere of your brain attributed to creativity. Ultimately, as you will begin to understand more fully in P2LR Step 9, these right-brain activities make the entire P2LR process more efficient and effective.

There are many benefits to developing a RPVS. For example, because your RPVS will articulate what your "ideal" self and life will look like, it will be easier to develop the goals, milestones, and strategies that will help you to realize your vision. A RPVS can also serve as a yardstick against which you can measure your current situation and your progress. Moreover, having a clear RPVS allows you to evaluate your values. If, for example, one of your values is integrity, you will know when you are compromising the fulfillment of your vision if you are acting without integrity. In other words, your RPVS will help guide the decisions you make and the directions you take.

Unlike a goal, once you have created it, your RPVS will rarely change. This is because it represents the very essence of who you are, who you want to become, and your reasons (your "WHYs") for the way you want to experience and see yourself and your future. In short, you are manufacturing a new perspective. When you adopt this new perspective, you will start to notice that your thoughts and behaviors will begin to align with this new outlook which, in turn, will help you begin to leave behind your old, irrational ways of thinking and acting.

For obvious and rational reasons, your RPVS should have a positive tone. This is because the way you see yourself and your future impacts everything you think and do. Above all, it impacts your level of happiness and sense of serenity.

If your vision of self and your future is depicted in negative ways, your thoughts, behaviors, and state of happiness will be impacted negatively. Conversely, if you choose to think or do things that cause you to see yourself and your future in more positive ways (e.g., rationally viewing your future as promising and yourself as someone who has potential), your state of happiness and serenity will be influenced in a positive direction.

This is the basis for labeling a negative vision of yourself or your future as irrational. Any effort you put into seeing yourself and your potential in a more positive light is a rational decision that will lead to increased happiness and success. This means that enduring happiness only comes to those who think and do what it takes to attain an image of themselves and their future that is rational, in that it increases rather than diminishes their sense of happiness, serenity, and overall success in life.

In addition to struggling with unhappiness, individuals who have an irrational view of themselves and their future have trouble achieving their goals because they are held back by their thinking, their perceived abilities, and their overall potential. According to self-image psychology, this means to do certain things you must see yourself as someone who can do those types of things. And, to see yourself doing certain things, you must become the kind of person who does those things. With this in mind, the goal of this step is to help you overcome and change limiting beliefs about yourself, your abilities, and your future potential by creating an RPVS that will enable you to become the kind of person who does the kinds of things you want to do in life.

> *We become what we want to be by consistently being what we want to become. Character is a manifestation of what you are becoming.*
> *- Richard G. Scott*

I have successfully used the techniques described in this step to help my clients 1) identify irrational beliefs about themselves and their future that limit their potential, and 2) replace these irrational beliefs with a Rational Personal Vision Statement (a mental prototype of how individuals view themselves and their future) that gives them a sense of hope and promise regarding themselves and their potential. This step will help you begin manufacturing and testing your RPVS as a means of deciding how you want and need to see yourself to achieve your full potential.

As you begin this process it is useful to remember that there are two fundamental, but interrelated, aspects to a RPVS. They include designing a prototype RPVS that represents the best possible person you can become (given the real, instead of the perceived, limits on your potential) while living the best possible life you can live. More specifically, the RPVS you develop and evaluate should represent what you want to become, do, feel, think, own, associate with, and impact by some date in the future.

When you reflect on the final version of your RPVS, it should remind you that this final "highest and best" version of yourself and your future must be rational in that it helps you achieve your goals, feel the way you want to feel, solve your problems and, above all, increase your state of happiness and sense of well-being. With this in mind, I have defined a RPVS as a conscious recognition and appraisal of your self and your future, grounded in the facts of reality, required to think and act in rational ways that promote personal and interpersonal growth and development, happiness, and serenity.

After using the techniques here to design, test, and enhance the various elements that make up your RPVS, you will eventually decide on a final version that you will, in turn, work to mentally assimilate using the techniques described in subsequent P2LR Steps.

Ideas for Implementing This Step & Mastering This Competency

This assignment will guide you through a process of designing and testing a Rational Personal Vision Statement (RPVS) using the "Rational Personal Vision Statement Guide" and then, help you evaluate and refine your RPVS until you have decided on a final version. Once you have finalized your RPVS and identified what adds to and takes away from it, you can begin to choose to think and act in ways that will cause you to realize everything you have outlined in your final RPVS.

Over time, as you decide to make additional changes, you will most likely need to revisit this statement. This is due to the fact that a necessary first step in true change requires making sure that you vision of self, or you self-image, is aligned with the things that you want to change about yourself. Once again, this is because you can do certain things unless you become the kind of person who does those kinds of things.

There are several steps in this process:

1. Ask yourself the following "Visioning Questions" to help you begin thinking about what you want to put into your RPVS:

- What inspires me? What do I want my life to stand for?
- If I could fix one problem in the world what would it be? What would I do about this problem?
- What are my most important values?
- What are the main things that motivate me/ bring me joy and satisfaction?
- What are the two best moments I have experienced in the past 10 years?
- What three things would I do if I won a 200 million dollar lottery?
- What are my greatest strengths/abilities/traits/ things I do best?
- What are at least two things I can start doing/do

more often that use my strengths and bring me joy?
- What are at least two things I can start thinking that will bring me greater happiness?
- What are at least two things I would like to stop doing or do as little as possible?
- If a miracle occurred and my life was just as I wanted it to be, what would be different?

2. Use the "Rational Personal Vision Statement Guide" to a) identify pictures or images that represent the things you want to BEcome, Do or Get—taken together, these images will represent your ideal RPVS; b) briefly explain how each image represents something you want; c) describe the reason "WHY" you want these things; and d) after you have described what you want and WHY, decide on one "Cue Word" that represents each of the images making up your RPVS.
3. Use the "RPVS Rationality Guide" to evaluate and identify elements in your RPVS that are irrational.

4. Revise the irrational elements in your RPVS.

5. Repeat steps 2 and 3 until all elements in your RPVS are rational.

After completing this assignment move on to the next P2LR step. The following steps will build on what you have done here by helping you refine, operationalize, and mentally assimilate your RPVS.

Rational Personal Vision Statement Guide

Identify 10 pictures or images that represent what you want to **BE, DO, GET**. After you have finished this step, these images will represent your Rational Personal Vision Statement. Briefly 1) explain how each image represents something you want to **BE** (calm, successful, thin, on time, confident, faithful, disciplined, fun, trustworthy, etc.), **DO** (graduate from college, get married, travel around the world, write a book, etc.) and **GET** (a new car or home, great job, a boat, etc.). Then describe the reason WHY you want the things represented by each picture. After you have described how you want to see yourself and your future, and WHY, decide on 1 "Cue-Word" that represents each of the images making up your PVS.

IMAGE 1	I want to...	The reasons WHY are...	Cue Word 1
IMAGE 2	I want to...	The reasons WHY are...	Cue Word 2
IMAGE 3	I want to...	The reasons WHY are...	Cue Word 3
IMAGE 4	I want to...	The reasons WHY are...	Cue Word 4
IMAGE 5	I want to...	The reasons WHY are...	Cue Word 5
IMAGE 6	I want to...	The reasons WHY are...	Cue Word 6
IMAGE 7	I want to...	The reasons WHY are...	Cue Word 7
IMAGE 8	I want to...	The reasons WHY are...	Cue Word 8
IMAGE 9	I want to...	The reasons WHY are...	Cue Word 9
IMAGE 10	I want to...	The reasons WHY are...	Cue Word 10

Table 10

RPVS RATIONALITY GUIDE

Ask each element (represented by an image and cue word) in your initial Rational Personal Vision Statement (RPVS) the following questions. If you answer no to any of these questions it's likely that the element you are considering is irrational. Revise the irrational elements until you can answer yes to every question. Feel free to add to or take away from the questions provided here.

If I fully adopt this element in my Rational Personal Vision Statement, will I:
• reach my full potential?

RPVS RATIONALITY GUIDE (continued)

- become the kind of person I want to be?
- achieve my short- and long-term goals?
- learn from my past, prepare for my future, and live in the present?
- have the ability to think and act in terms of principles and not emotions?
- perceive myself as someone who is in control of my destiny?
- be able to solve my problems and ask others for help when I need it?
- feel secure about who I am, and not feel insecure when others question how I see myself and live my life?
- be able to evaluate what others think and feel against my own standards, and have the courage to act according to my own convictions, regardless of what others do or say?
- feel secure enough about my beliefs that I can change them in the face of new facts?
- be able to exercise self-control by stoping, thinking, and making rational decisions?
- look beyond the surface, find real meaning, and weigh the pros and cons of an event or issue?
- wait for things that I want even when this requires patience and delaying immediate gratification?
- keep trying, even when things don't go the way I would like them to?
- see myself as someone who is equal in value to others, rather than inferior or superior, while accepting differences in my abilities, socio-economic standing, and personal potential?
- respect and obey the laws that are rational in that they are fair and just?
- respect the dignity of all men and women, without respect to religion, race, or gender?

Table 11

MY PLAN FOR P2LR STEP 4

How will I need to see myself to change or become the kind of person who consistently accomplishes these things (add elements to my RPVS)?

P2LR STEP 5
Set Rational Goals

Step 5 will guide you in setting and evaluating goals that are directly relevant to your Rational Personal Vision Statement (RPVS). Specifically, the purposes of this step are to help you 1) begin to operationalize your RPVS by guiding you through the process of setting a single goal for each RPVS element, 2) evaluate the rationality of your goals, and 3) determine whether or not you are ready to achieve the goals you plan to set.

In short, goals are written statements that explain what you want to obtain or accomplish within a certain period of time. Good goals are specific, measurable, realistic, and stated in terms of a specific time period.

When I set goals I ask myself six questions. These questions help me operationalize what I plan to accomplish and by when.

Six Questions to Writing Goals

1) Am I committed to this goal? If I am not committed to achieving the goal, it goes in the trash. If I am, the likelihood that I will achieve it is in the high 90% range. Why set a goal if you are not committed to doing what it takes to achieve it?

2) What do I plan to accomplish? If I have a clear idea about what I am trying to accomplish, I will have a much better idea as to whether or not I can do what it takes to achieve the goal. If I do not have a precise understanding of where I am going and what I am going to do, I probably will not get there.

3) What will I need to do to prepare to achieve this goal? Getting prepared before I launch into a goal-achieving mode is crucial. I typically spend at least 10 days getting ready. This includes doing everything that is described in Steps 6, 7, and 8 in the P2LR process, which involves making a plan of action and visualizing how I will succeed before I begin the hard work of succeeding.

4) When will I start and finish? Setting a start and finish date is exciting for me. For example, if I plan to write a book I spend several days deciding on what it will take to write the book and how long. In the case of this book, I gave myself from September 18, 2012, to January 2nd, 2013. Although it was a very ambitious schedule, it was realistic because I had already put together most of the material I wanted to write about.

5) What barriers may I encounter when trying to achieve this goal? Answering this question helps me anticipate the people, places, or things that may prevent me from achieving my goal. This information helps me plan what I will need to think and/or do differently to overcome barriers to successfully achieving my objective. (Step 7

will provide you specific guidance on how to approach this question more strategically.)

6) How will I know if I succeed and achieve my goal? As I mentioned in the beginning of this book, I like to follow the quote by Covey: "Start with the end in mind." If I can see the outcome of my work and the outcome is a good one, I am motivated by this vision of my success. In the case of this book, I could see the book being advertised and sold on Amazon. I could see many people benefiting from the principles in the book. And, I could see my work becoming more efficient and effective with my clients and students by readily referring to these principles in session and in the classroom.

The second of the six questions that I ask myself before embarking on a goal, "What do I plan to accomplish?," also relates to the type of goal I plan to set. There are many different types of goals, including BE, KNOW, DO, FEEL, and ACQUIRE GOALS. For example, you can set 1) BE GOALS, to become more confident, self-disciplined, patient, trustworthy, or assertive; 2) KNOW GOALS, to learn more about your spouse, automobiles, a profession, or cooking; 3) DO GOALS, to accomplish something, like finishing a gardening project, losing weight, or exercising four times per week; 4) FEEL GOALS, to feel differently (less angry or more committed) about someone or something, like your job, your spouse, your living circumstances, or a wayward child; and/or 5) ACQUIRE GOALS, to get something you want that you do not currently have, like a new car, a home, an honor at work, a big screen television, or a boat. Once again, in this step each goal should relate back to one of the elements in your RPVS.

A good way to start the process of thinking about the types of goals you should set here (most are "BE GOALS') is to answer the following questions in terms of how they relate to each Rational Self Perception or RSP element. As you answer each question, you will begin to see what you need to do differently (more or less of) to make your RPVS a reality.

- What do I need to think more about to make this element in my RPVS a reality?
- What do I need to think less about to make this element in my RPVS a reality?
- What do I need to do more of to make this element in my RPVS a reality?
- What do I need to do less of to make this element in my RPVS a reality?
- Where do I need to spend more time to make this element in my RPVS a reality?
- Where do I need to spend less time to make this element in my RPVS a reality?
- Who should I spend more time with to make this element in my RPVS a reality?
- Who should I spend less time with to make this element in my RPVS a reality?
- What will prevent me from thinking and doing

the things required to make this element in my RPVS a reality?

Once again, the purpose of this step is to help you begin to operationalize your RPVS by guiding you through the process of setting a single goal for each RPVS element. The goals you set will help you become someone different than you currently are by helping you re-engineer how you see yourself and your future. The reasoning behind this idea is that you simply cannot do certain things in life unless you become the kind of person who does those kinds of things.

During my last visit to China in 2011, I made several presentations on a book my wife and I published in 2001 that had to do with character education. One of the speakers who was also invited by the Chinese to speak was Dr Stan Weed. I was fascinated by Dr Weed's work and the character and skill traits he recommended that Chinese schools and parents teach their children. I have included these traits below as an example of some of the BE GOALS you may consider as you formulate a goal for each element in your RPVS (Weed, 2013).

> • I want to BE someone who is committed to Worth and Potential in all people. In this case, worth means that everyone is important and has value. Potential means having unique capacities and abilities that we can develop.

> • I want to BE someone who is committed to the

Rights and Responsibilities of all people, with the understanding that 1) rights are what all people are given at birth (choices and opportunities) or earn by working hard, and 2) a responsibility is a duty, especially the duty to make good choices. Rights are inseparable from responsibilities and can be lost when we make bad choices or violate the rights of others.

• I want to BE someone who is committed to Fairness and Justice, meaning that I act toward others without bias or prejudice, and respect the rights, worth, and potential of others. It also means seeking solutions to problems that are objective and impartial, ensuring that consequences are appropriate for the behavior.

• I want to BE someone who is committed to Care and Consideration. This means I will show kindness and empathy in my actions. It requires personal acceptance of the basic principle of inherent worth and potential and giving full regard to the rights and worth of others.

• I want to BE someone who is committed to Effort and Excellence. This means I will work hard and persevere until a task is completed. It means not giving up because it is difficult and striving to achieve the best possible quality.

• I want to BE someone who is committed to

Social Responsibility. This means I will make choices and take actions that will have a positive effect on other people and our world, both now and in the future.

• I want to BE someone who has Personal Integrity. This means I will have an uncompromising adherence to standards of ethical behavior regardless of external pressures. This means doing the right thing no matter what others do or say.

• I want to BE someone who has Self-Control. This means I will be able to stop, think, and make good decisions.

• I want to BE someone who exercises Delayed Gratification. This means I will be able to wait for the things that I want while respecting the fact that attaining many of the best things in life require effort, time, and patience.

• I want to BE someone who has Persistence. This is the ability to keep trying, even when things do not go the way we would like them to. It means not giving up when the task is difficult. Persistence recognizes small successes.

• I want to BE a Critical Thinker. This means that I will learn to look beyond the surface, find real meaning, and weigh the pros and cons of an event or issue.

• I want to BE someone who is Resistant to Peer Pressure. This is the influence others have on me. It can be positive, negative, or both. Coping with Peer Pressure means being able to weigh what others think and feel against my own standards. It means having the courage to act according to my own convictions, regardless of what others do or say.

• I want to BE someone who can effectively implement Conflict Resolution. This means that I will be able to solve problems that come up through communicating, negotiating, and/or compromising.

• I want to BE someone who can Prioritize Competing Standards. This means I will be able to make the better choice when two ethical choices are in conflict.

• I want to BE someone who Sets and Achieves Worthy Goals. In this case, I will prepare for my future by setting meaningful and measureable goals that I can reach.

My fascination with the above BE GOALS is partly due to the work of happiness researchers Dr Ed Deiner and Dr Martin Seligman who both agree that character and skill traits are important predictors of happiness. The other and, perhaps more important, reason is that it is completely irrational to assume that someone who does not have basic character and value traits such as respect for others rights, self-discipline, delayed gratification, and persistence, can be happy and serene in our modern society. You can test this idea for yourself by completing the following assignment.

Although BE goals are important, you will recall that your RPVS is more than becoming, it also has to do with your desires and aspirations to learn, do, and acquire things. This means, as was mentioned in Step 4, that you will also need to set goals that represent what you want to do, feel, think, own, associate with, and impact by some date in the future. To help stimulate the kind of thinking you need to engage in to formulate different types of goals, you can ask yourself some of the following questions:

- How would I like things to be different in my life?
- If a miracle occurred and everything in my life was the way I think it should be, what would be different?
- What do I want to achieve in life that I have not yet achieved?
- What do I want more of?
- What do I want less of?
- What will be different and by when?

Listed are some sample generic goals that relate to how you might respond to these questions: to develop better self-esteem and self-understanding; to feel better about myself or others; to be/feel more "balanced"; to "get better" at something; to unlearn (or substitute) new habits or old ones; to learn how to communicate better with others (on the job and in relationships); to learn how to set and achieve goals; to control my appetite; to learn not to lay blame elsewhere, or to learn to be more responsible myself; to overcome or solve a particular problem, and/or to forgive or forget—or both; to stop acting out fears and needs with others; to overcome depression or anxiety or uncontrolled anger, etc.

Are You Ready to Achieve Your Goals?

There is a saying, "You must be, before you can do." As I have stressed before, this means if you plan to do certain things, you must become the kind of person who does those kinds of things. This step will help you determine what you need to think and do to realize your vision and achieve your goals. It will also help you evaluate your readiness to change.

As explained in Section II, the ability to achieve any goal requires 1) believing you are someone who can achieve the goal, and 2) actually being someone who has what it takes to achieve the goal. Both of these conditions are necessary.. To achieve, you must both believe and have what is required to achieve.

In addition to helping you set goals, Step 5 will help you 1) decide whether or not you believe and have what it takes to accomplish these things, and 2) in the case where you do not believe or do not have what it takes to achieve your goals, begin the process of determining what you need to think or do differently to make up for these deficiencies.

Ideas for Implementing This Step & Mastering This Competency

The purposes of Step 5 are to help you 1) begin to operationalize your Rational Personal Vision Statement (RPVS) by guiding you through the process of setting a single goal for each RPVS element; 2) evaluate the rationality of your goals; and 3) start to determine whether or not you are ready to achieve the goals you plan to set. Although the part of this step that involves assessing your readiness is somewhat redundant and may seem like "overkill," it is not. Taking a very close look at a goal before you set and start working toward the goal is key to achieving the goal. In fact, I am of the opinion that you should never set a goal that you do not plan to achieve. This process will help you decide whether the goals you set are ones that you really want to do and help you determine what it takes to achieve the goals.

1. Use the "RPVS Goal Guide" below to write down at least one goal for each element in your RPVS. Be precise and only include goals that you are committed to and confident that you can attain. For ideas about the type, content, and format of each goal, refer to the "Six Questions for Writing

Goals" listed at the beginning of this step. In addition, refer to the questions from the Hapiness Algorithm Planner (in Section I) relating to what you need to think or do more or less of, which will help you to realize your RPVS.

2. For each goal you set using the "RPVS Goal Guide," ask yourself the following questions:

- Do I believe I can achieve this goal?

- Do I have what it takes to achieve the goal (e.g., knowledge, skills, resources, support)?

- Based on my responses to the last question, what do I need to think or do to get what I need to accomplish each goal?

3. To assess and begin building your motivation to achieve each goal, ask yourself these questions:

- Why do I want to achieve this particular goal?

- What good things may happen if I achieve this goal?

- What bad things may happen if I do not reach this goal?

- How will things be different if I achieve this goal?

4. (a) To further assess your readiness, including how committed you are, how confident you are, and how prepared you are, you can ask yourself the following questions for each goal:

• How committed am I that I can achieve this goal? (circle number)

(no commitment) 0 -- 1 -- 2 -- 3 -- 4 -- 5 -- 6 -- 7 -- 8 -- 9 -- 10 (totally committed)

• How confident am I that I can achieve this goal? (circle number)

(no confidence) 0 -- 1 -- 2 -- 3 -- 4 -- 5 -- 6 -- 7 -- 8 -- 9 -- 10 (totally confident)

• How prepared are you to achieve this goal? (circle number)

(no preparation) 0 -- 1 -- 2 -- 3 -- 4 -- 5 -- 6 -- 7 -- 8 -- 9 -- 10 (totally prepared)

5. (b) What do you need to raise each number you circled to a 10?

6. What else do you need to achieve the goal? Improved self-image, knowledge, skills, social support, money?

RPVS GOAL GUIDE

Use this form to write down at least one goal for each element in your Rational Personal Vision Statement (RPVS). Be precise and only include goals that you are committed to, confident that you can attain, and are congruent with your RPVS.

| CUE 1 |
| CUE 2 |
| CUE 3 |
| CUE 4 |
| CUE 5 |
| CUE 6 |
| CUE 7 |
| CUE 8 |
| CUE 9 |
| CUE 10 |

Table 12

MY PLAN FOR P2LR STEP 5

What are my short-, medium-, and long-term goals?

P2LR STEP 6

Determine What Will Motivate You to Change and Grow

One of my clients who was resisting the need to change some behaviors that were interfering with his marriage and work once said to me in a therapy session, "I probably won't change until the problem gets bigger than the solution." I said "Yes, that's the way many addicts think things must play out; however, there is another option which is to make the solution bigger and better than the problem." In other words, you can hold on to a bad habit until things get so unbearable that you must change or, you can create another form of motivation that does not involve so much unnecessary suffering. For example, you can wait to experience the pain of quitting smoking until you get the diagnosis of lung cancer, which inevitably results in great pain, or you can motivate yourself to go through the pain of quitting before your health fails.

Step 6 will help you understand the principle of motivation and how you can use different motivation techniques to increase your desire to start and persist in activities that you would not normally engage in.

First, motivation is defined as an internal drive that activates and maintains goal-oriented behaviors. It involves internal and external forces that cause us to act, whether it is eating to satisfy hunger, exercising to lose weight, going to college to improve the chances at getting a good job, or reading a book to gain additional knowledge.

Motivation has three major components. These include activation, persistence, and intensity.

Activation involves the decision to initiate a behavior, such as exercise. This could entail deciding to jog at a local park for thirty minutes, four days per week.

Persistence is the ongoing effort toward a goal even though obstacles such as time, energy, and resources may exist. For example, if the weather turned bad for an extended period of time and prevented you from jogging at the park, a person with persistence would join a fitness center to run on a treadmill even though this may require investing in a gym membership.

Intensity is the necessary focus and consistency that goes into pursuing a goal. While one person who sets the goal to jog at the park may walk instead, another person may strive to improve the time it takes to complete the jog by increasing the pace of the run.

The factors that most often diminish motivation are the lack of confidence, focus, and direction. As you may have already discovered, the P2LR steps inherently attack these motivation killers by helping you believe you can succeed, determine specifically what you want, and provide direction toward your end goals, respectively.

The previous step (Step 5), where you both set and analyzed goals, was also designed to help you build motivation by asking you to identify and visualize the benefits (positive outcomes) you expect to gain from making this change, as well as the negative outcomes you could face if you do not reach your goals. As you may have noticed, this simple exercise has proven to be effective in building motivation to remain focused on what you want to accomplish.

Another important consideration in building and sustaining motivation is to make sure your thoughts are congruent with your goals. To this end, Step 10 will teach you how to monitor and master your internal monologue in a way that ensures that your thoughts are congruent with and in support of what you are trying to accomplish. For obvious reasons, specific positive self-statements will help strengthen your motivation to persist.

Understanding and Applying Extrinsic Motivation

Motivation is often described as being either intrinsic or extrinsic. Intrinsic motivations are those that arise from within you. It is your desire to do something because it is enjoyable to you, like reading a book or watching television or going to a movie. My daughter-in-law and son enjoy watching cooking demonstrations on television because they enjoy cooking together. I like to ride young horses for the sake of the challenge. My wife is intrinsically motivated to shop for items that can improve the appearance of our home. Again, intrinsic motivation comes from within because you want to do a good job at something because it is something that you want for yourself. That is, if you are intrinsically motivated, the enjoyment you experience is sufficient for you to want to perform the activity in the future.

A person who is intrinsically motivated may volunteer to provide service to needy persons in the community because it makes him or her feel good to make a difference. At the same time, other people may join in the same cause because they believe it will make them look good in the eyes of others in the community. The second example is one of extrinsic motivation.

Extrinsic motivations are those that arise from outside yourself. This type of motivation reflects a desire to do something because of external rewards. Individuals who are extrinsically motivated often engage in activities that they do not enjoy because they believe they will be somehow rewarded for their efforts. In other words, it is your desire to doing something because there is something in it for you, whether or not you feel a sense of accomplishment.

For example, a person who works at a job that she dislikes to earn more money than a lesser paying job that she enjoys is extrinsically motivated. Another example of an individual who is extrinsically motivated is a person who decides to major in something he does not enjoy in college, like medicine or law, simply because he can earn more money and gain more status than if he had majored in a less prestigious subject that he enjoyed.

The reason for making the distinction between the two types of motivation is because they can be applied in different ways to increase activation, persistence, and intensity toward a specific goal. Because external motivation is easier to manufacture than intrinsic motivation, this P2LR step guides you in how to systematically create extrinsic motivation around your goals using what researcher refer to as the "Premack Principle" (Premack, 1965). This principle is based on the idea that any high-probability behavior (things you really like to do) can be used to reinforce a low-probability behavior (things you do not like to do).

The Premack Principle has a number of practical advantages that can help you motivate yourself. For example, if you want to motivate yourself to do something you are not likely to do (a low-probability behavior), like exercise every morning before work, you must make a high-probability behavior like going out with friends or taking a vacation contingent (dependent) upon the low-probability behavior. "Yes, I will give myself a quick trip to the Bahamas next month if I first [the contingency] get up and exercise before work for an hour, at least four days week, for the entire month of January."

In psychological literature, the Premack Principle is applied in a motivational learning theory called "Operant Conditioning." This theory relies on the principles of contingency, reinforcement, and shaping in the process of motivating compliance with desired actions (Cole, Friedman & Bagwell, 1986).

The principle of contingency suggests that, as is implied by the above example, you are more likely to follow through on a goal and a plan of action when the things you like to do are dependent (contingent) upon the performance of things you do not necessarily enjoy doing. For example: "Hey self, you may NOT hang out with friends this weekend unless you work out for at least one hour before work on Monday, Tuesday, Thursday and Friday [a low probability behavior]."

On a day-to-day basis, many consequences are contingent upon behavior. For example, getting paid is contingent upon working; physical alertness is contingent upon the amount of rest you get; knowledge is dependent upon the amount of training and experience a person has. The concept of contingency is important here because it is used in connection with reinforcement (Cautela & Kastenbaum, 1995; Cole, Friedman & Bagwell, 1986) to motivate the performance of assigned duties.

Reinforcement is a principle that refers to the presentation of an event or stimuli, which, in turn, results in an increase in the frequency of a desired behavior. There are two types of reinforcement: positive and negative.

A "Positive Reinforcer" is distinguished by its specific effect on the desired behavior. If you give yourself a reinforcer—like a trip to the Bahamas—in connection with a behavior you do not necessarily want to engage in— exercising before work—and exercise behavior increases, then the trip is a positive reinforcer. Hence, the defining characteristic of a positive reinforcer is its ability to increase the desired behavior it follows, like exercising more or eating less.

The term "reward" is often used synonymously with positive reinforcer. However, in the strictest sense, a reward is not a positive reinforcer unless it actually increases the frequency of a desired behavior. If, for example, you reward yourself with money for exercising and you do not exercise as planned, the monetary reward was not a positive reinforcer.

Some examples of reinforcers I have used to successfully increase desired behaviors include the following: buy a new CD or book; watch a movie; spend an hour riding my horse; get a massage; take a walk with my wife in the park; take a day off work; listen to some of my favorite music; take a nap; take a day off from one of my goal activities; or invite friends over for a small gathering.

The principle of positive reinforcement carries a strong message: if I can identify and implement positive reinforcers, I can motivate myself to perform desired, low-probability behaviors. And the stronger the reinforcer, the more motivated I will become. Therefore, key to motivating myself is my ability to identify and apply strong reinforcers.

Once you have identified your individual reinforcers, it becomes possible to use them as a basis for motivating yourself toward specific goals. Formulating a reinforcement schedule that is designed to apply these principles can help with this process.

A reinforcement schedule can either be continuous or intermittent in nature. Continuous reinforcement requires reinforcing an event every time it occurs. In contrast, intermittent reinforcement requires reinforcing only after you have done something once. For example, giving yourself a reinforcer every time you work on your goals is a continuous reinforcement; but reinforcing yourself once per week, after you have done everything you planned to do on your goals during that week you work on your goals every day (the contingency), is an intermittent reinforcer.

In most instances, continuous and intermittent reinforcement schedules produce important differences in the performance of desired behavior. For example, during the initial stages of engaging in a new behavior, continuous reinforcement is more likely to motivate early performance.

Many times, reinforcing a single response cannot motivate a desired behavior. This is due to a number of factors, such as the complexity of the behavior, the intensity of the behavior, and the duration of the goal. In such instances, I suggest the use of another operant conditioning principle called shaping.

"Shaping" a desired behavior involves reinforcing small steps, or approximations, toward a desired action rather than reinforcing only the desired response. The final desired behavior is eventually achieved through the reinforcement of successful approximations that resemble the final response. For example, if you plan to lose 50 pounds over twelve months, you may want to reward yourself in stages

1) in terms of number of pounds lost (reinforcing the loss of the first 10 pounds); or 2) for faithful adherence to a particular weight loss approach (eating less than 20 grams of fat per day for a week); or 3) for consistently following a planned exercise routine for a set amount of time (exercise for 30 minutes per day, 5 days per week, for 2 weeks). In this case you are setting up a contingency schedule that reinforces loss of the first 10 pounds, eating less fat per day for a week, and exercising faithfully for two weeks. This is an example of "shaping" which involves setting small goals that are an approximation of, and that lead to, the end goal, which is to lose 50 pounds in a year.

Once again, all of the steps in the P2LR process are inherently designed to help build motivation. The plan for building motivation in this step is to systematically manufacture extrinsic motivation using operant conditioning. This strategy is outlined in the following implementation plan.

Ideas for Implementing This Step & Mastering This Competency

1. List and spend some time visualizing positive outcomes you expect to gain from making this change to motivate you to remain focused on what you want to accomplish.

2. List and spend time visualizing the negative outcomes you could face if you do not make this change to motivate you to remain focused on what you do want to accomplish.

3. Make a list of positive reinforcers. Consider things other than food and alcohol that you will reward yourself with if you do what you plan to do.

4. Use the "CCS Reinforcement Guide" to develop a plan to reinforce the goals or activities you know you will have difficulty motivating yourself to do without applying an extrinsic reward. In column 1 list the goals you plan to reinforce. In column 2, list subgoals or activities that will help you achieve the goal in column 1. Finally, in column 3 list the specific reinforcer that is contingent upon doing the things you listed in column 2.

5. Evaluate your progress. If you are not doing what you plan to do, the things you have designated as reinforcers are not reinforcing. Remember, the defining characteristic of a reinforcer is that it increases the behavior it is contingent upon.

CCS REINFORCEMENT GUIDE

Goals I Plan to Reinforce	Subgoal or Goal-Related Activity I Plan to Reinforce	What is the Reinforcer? How and When Will I Reinforce My Success?

Table 12

MY PLAN FOR P2LR STEP 6

> ### What will motivate me to achieve my goals?

P2LR STEP 7

Identify and Anticipate Triggers and Barriers to Change and Growth

In addition to helping you think about and set goals, the previous step (Step 6) was also designed to help you start thinking about the barriers to achieving a goal, including lack of motivation, confidence, preparation, etc. This step (Step 7) will define both triggers and barriers in more detail and explain how they can undermine your ability to realize your Rational Personal Vision Statment (RPVS) and reach your goals.

Although there are innumerable triggers and barriers, with training and practice, you can readily identify, anticipate, and rationally cope with triggers and overcome barriers. With this in mind, this step will help you 1) understand what triggers are and their role in irrational thoughts and behaviors; 2) think about and prepare to avoid or respond more rationally to the triggers that have caused you problems in the past; and 3) identify, anticipate, and prepare to overcome barriers that may prevent you from making progress toward realizing your RPVS and achieving your goals.

Behavioral Triggers: What Are They and Why Are They Important?

We all have triggers that are unique to us and our own circumstances. Irrational triggers are those things that lead to a chain of undesired thoughts, feelings, and behaviors. Fortunately, triggers can be identified, anticipated, and controlled. This step offers a recognize-avoid-cope approach commonly used in cognitive behavioral therapy, which will help you recognize and change irrational thinking patterns and reactions. It also provides a step-by-step process that will help you uncover the type and nature of your triggers and to make a plan for handling them. With time, and by practicing new responses, you will find that your unwanted triggers will lose strength, and you will gain confidence in your ability to counter irrational triggers, urges, thoughts, physical sensations, or emotions that tempt you to think or act against your self-interest.

Recognize Two Types of "Triggers"

Anything that sets off a chain reaction of predictable behaviors can be considered either a rational or irrational trigger. "Rational triggers" are people, places, and things that prompt you to think and act in ways that help strengthen your commitment to health, happiness, and serenity. Conversely, anything that causes a chain reaction resulting in irrational thoughts or actions is an "irrational trigger."

Triggers can also be labeled as external or internal. "External Triggers" are people, places, things, or times of day that offer opportunities or remind you of a behavior you are trying to overcome, like smoking, overeating, or drug abuse. These high-risk situations are more obvious, predictable, and avoidable than internal triggers.

Because it is easier to avoid a trigger than it is to cope with a trigger, the best initial strategy for dealing with external triggers is to avoid people, places, and things that typically trigger urges and irrational thoughts and actions that are incongruent with your goals. After you have become more competent in your ability to identify and rationally deal with triggers, you may decide to ease gradually into some situations you now choose to avoid.

"Internal Triggers" can be puzzling because the urge to think or act irrationally seems to just "pop up." However, if you develop the knowledge and skills required to pause and think about it when it happens, you will be able to identify some ingrained beliefs that come past experience. For example, these internal triggers may be linked to living with and being raised by irrational caretakers, being schooled by irrational teachers, and/or buying into irrational ideas propagated by politicians or marketers or certain religious leaders or television programming.

The fact is, because we do not live in a perfectly rational society, all of us have been socialized in a way that has caused us, at one time or another, to embrace false beliefs that can trigger irrational thoughts, urges, emotional pain, and frustration. In recognition of this fact, behavioral scientists have identified, classified, and labeled these internal triggers with various names, including irrational beliefs, cognitive distortions, and thought viruses.

Irrational Beliefs as Triggers and Barriers

Albert Ellis, the father of Rational Emotive Behavioral Therapy, has studied and identified 11 common beliefs that trigger irrational thoughts that consistently undermine happiness and serenity. He labels these Irrational Beliefs. 1) It is a dire necessity for me to be loved or approved by almost all others who are significant to me; 2) I must be thoroughly competent, adequate, and achieving, in all important respects in order to be worthwhile; 3) The world must be fair. People must act fairly and considerately, and if they do not, they are bad, wicked, villainous, or incredibly stupid; they should be severely blamed and punished; 4) It is awful and terrible when things are not the way I very much want them to be; 5) There is not much I can do about my anxiety, anger, depression, or unhappiness because my feelings are caused by what happens to me; 6) If something is dangerous or dreadful, I should be constantly and excessively upset about it and should dwell on the possibility of it occurring; 7) It is easier to avoid and to put off facing life's difficulties and responsibilities than face them; 8) I'm quite dependent on others and need someone stronger than myself to rely upon; I can't run my own life; 9) My past history mainly causes my present feelings and behavior; things from my past, which once strongly influenced me, will always strongly influence me; 10) I must become very anxious, angry, or depressed over someone else's problems and disturbances if I care about that person; and 11) There is a right and perfect solution to almost all problems, and it is awful not to find it.

David Burns, in his popular book, Feeling Good (1980), labels these beliefs that trigger irrational thoughts, urges, and unpleasant emotions "Cognitive Distortions." He also identifies the most problematic Cognitive Distortions: 1) All or Nothing Thinking - thinking in black and white when many legitimate alternatives exist; 2) Over-Generalization - pretending that everything can be judged by a single occurrence or person. Trying to "tar everything with the same brush;" 3) Mental Filter - seeing only the bad so you lose your perspective. Not widening your focus; 4) Disqualifying the Positive - As it says, this is the way the mind justifies inner-philosophies that make you unhappy; 5) Jumping to Conclusions (a) Mind Reader Error - assuming people think a certain thing when you have no evidence for that, (b) Fortune-Telling Error - assuming that a certain thing will happen when you have no evidence for that; 6) Magnification or Minimalization - blowing things out of proportion or minimalizing the good aspects in yourself or a situation; 7) Emotional Reasoning - taking things personally when they were not meant that way; 8) Should Statement - feeling things should be a certain way that you think best and letting it get to you when they are not; 9) Labeling or Mislabeling - labeling yourself or someone else, rather than seeing them for the whole person they are; and 10) Personalization - thinking that things turn bad because you yourself are bad.

Donald Lofland, in his book titled Thought Viruses: Powerful Ways to Change Your Thought Patterns and Get What You Want in Life (1998), calls beliefs that cause irrationality, "Thought Viruses." In keeping with the writings of Ellis and Burns, Lofland states that we all have "unconscious thought patterns that distort our thinking and perception of the world." He also correctly states that these thought patters ". . . arise out of our learned behaviors and disempowering beliefs, and they can have a crippling effect on our professional and personal lives."

My own research related to internal triggers has revealed that individuals are triggered to start thinking about stories they tell themselves. These stories, sometimes called "Life Scripts" in the psychological literature, are influenced by our experiences with the people we are influenced by during our developmental years—our parents, teachers, and others. They help us live in and make sense of the world. They are both conscious and unconscious. And, what is most important here, these stories are both rational and irrational. The good news is that you can become aware of the conscious stories, and the irrational stories can be changed to rational ones.

Once again, irrational beliefs, whether conscious or unconscious, can serve as internal triggers that cause us harm and stand as barriers to rational living. They prevent us from thinking and living rationally. The good news here is that we can identify, anticipate, and counter thought viruses through techniques like cognitive restructuring and life script restructuring.

Barriers to Change

One wise person said, "When you focus on the barriers, you have taken your eye off the goal." No matter what goal you set, there are going to be barriers that you must overcome to reach the goal. The permutations and combinations of barriers are enumerable. The important thing is to understand they exist and must be dealt with if you hope to consistently reach your goals.

Common barriers to change and self improvement include lack of knowledge, false information, fear of asking for help, skill deficits, lack of commitment, procrastination, limited perspective, fear of failure, cognitive dissonance, seeing yourself as a victim or external locus of control, lack of discipline, physical disability (like no arms or legs or inability to see or hear), pessimistic friends or family members, denial, negative influences like television, lack of focus, insufficient desire, inability to deal with setbacks and disappointment, absence of passionate goals, inadequate resources, lack of confidence, self-limiting beliefs (like self-loathing, indecision, low self-esteem), destructive personal habits like substance abuse, regrets about the past, irrational thoughts, negative self-talk, pressures at work and at home, and lack of support. Several of these barriers are listed in Table 13. In column 2 I have provided some basic information about what the barrier is and what you can do about it.

Common Barriers	What IT Is and What You Can Do About IT
Lack of Knowledge	If you do not know how to do what you want to do, you will struggle. Read a book, search online, or ask someone who has the knowledge about the questions you need answers to.
False Information	Myths are popular everywhere. Do not be a victim. Take the time to make sure the information you are relying on is based on truth and not someone's wild guess or a crazy tradition that serves no good purpose other than to keep people in line. To remind my clients of this fact I tell them, "Any fool can create a myth and any fool can believe it. Check out your information before you buy in to a lie that costs you more than you are willing to pay."
Fear of Asking for Help	Do an online search, using Google, Bing, Yahoo, or YouTube.

Table 13

Common Barriers	What IT Is and What You Can Do About IT
Belief that You Must Learn Everything from Experience	One wise person said, "Experience is dear, but a fool learns by no other way." Learning from the "collective wisdom" of those who have gone before you is a much more efficient way of learning than having to learn everything by experience. Surely, you do not have to get cancer from smoking before you understand that tobacco use is the number one leading cause of preventable death and for every person who dies prematurely, 20 people are permanently injured by smoking. And surely, you do not believe that every cancer doctor (oncologist) must be a cancer survivor before they can practice their profession.
Skill Deficit	If you do not have the skills required to do what you want to do, you must do what is required to gain the skills.
Procrastination	Procrastination is the act of replacing high-priority actions with tasks of lower priority. It results from a lack of self-control and the inability to accurately predict how well you will perform tasks that you have put off until the last minute. It often leads to a decreased success in attaining your goals. A good way to challenge and overcome this bad habit is to only set goals and record actions steps that you are willing to follow through on. This makes the case for breaking down larger goals into small approximations of a larger goal.

Table 13

Common Barriers	What IT Is and What You Can Do About IT
Lack of Perspective	If you have never been out of your hometown, or have never met a person who has made significant changes in life, or have been raised by parents who are pessimists, or have been taught by people without any vision, you may suffer from lack of perspective. To overcome this, take a trip to another state or country, start and complete something you have never done before, watch science-based programming, look at the stars and ponder the immensity of the universe until you begin to realize that you have possibilities far beyond what you have ever imagined. I also suggest that you read the stories about Nick and Kyle below.
Fear of Failure	I often say the best predictor of the future is the past. To overcome a past that included failure, you must begin to create a present that will result in a past filled with success rather than failures. After all, if you succeed at something today, tomorrow you can look back at today (the past), and point to a success. This can be accomplished by setting small, achievable goals that are stepping-stones to your larger objectives. After all, nothing is preventing you from setting a goal right now that you can accomplish within minutes that will, in turn, help you achieve your larger goals.

Table 13

Common Barriers	What IT Is and What You Can Do About IT
Value- and Change-Based Cognitive Dissonance	"Cognitive Dissonance" (coined by Lester Festinger in 1956) is a sense of emotional discomfort when you simultaneously hold two or more conflicting cognitions: ideas, beliefs, values, or self-image. There are two types of cognitive dissonance: value-based and change-based. "Value-Based Cognitive Dissonance," which in religious terms is called guilt, is an emotional discomfort you experience when you think or do things that are inconsistent with what you believe to be "the right thing to think or do," like disobeying one of the ten commandments if you had a Judeo-Christian upbringing, or smoking the first cigarette if you grew up believing that smoking is dangerous, or engaging in sex before marriage if you believe that it is wrong. This type of dissonance can have a significant impact on self-esteem in that those who think and behave in ways that are inconsistent with their core values may experience a corresponding decrease in self-esteem. "Change-Based Cognitive Dissonance" occurs when you think and do things that are different than things you have thought and done in the past, like starting to exercise when you have not exercised in the past, or moving from a country where you drive on the right side of the road to a country where you drive on the left side. With both types of dissonance, the greater the discrepancy between the way you think things "should be," the greater discomfort you will experience. Both forms of dissonance must be understood and dealt with when making significant changes in your life. Both kinds of Cognitive Dissonance serve as an internal gauge that let you know when there is a "tremor in the force." As you become more mindful using the

Table 13

Common Barriers	What IT Is and What You Can Do About IT
Value- and Change-Based Cognitive Dissonance (continued)	techniques in P2LR Step 9, the "Uh Oh, Feeling" (dissonance) will help you consciously stop and ask yourself some very helpful questions. For example, when you experience dissonance you can stop and ask yourself the question, "Is this new thing I am thinking or doing congruent with my core beliefs?" If your answer is, "Yes," you can say to yourself, "Oh well, this uncomfortable feeling is normal and it will pass with time." On the other hand, if your answer to this question is, "No," you can do what is necessary to bring about congruence. The most "rational" way of dealing with dissonance is to identify and address thoughts and behaviors that are inconsistent with your desired self-image, goals, and plan of action.
Seeing Yourself as a Victim or Having an External Locus of Control	Viewing yourself as a victim of circumstances takes away your power to do something about the things that happen to you on a day-to-day basis. A victim mentality is a form of negative self-fulfilling prophecy. That is, if you always think you are a victim, you will continually end up being a victim of your own negativity. What is important in psychological well-being is not what happens to you, but how you deal with it. Those who believe otherwise have an external locus of control and tend to suffer considerably more than those who decide that they are in control of how they react to the things around them.

Table 13

Common Barriers	What IT Is and What You Can Do About IT
Lack of Self-Discipline	"A simple reality which is ignored at a terrible price is that most human misery can be prevented by wise and disciplined living," Victor Brown. Self-discipline is a learned skill that leads to ultimate freedom. Although most marketers and teenagers will tell you otherwise, the only people who are truly free are those who are totally self-disciplined. This is because they can get out of bed when they want to, start and finish projects, keep their wits about them under pressure, and control their temper when it needs to be controlled. Poor time management, poor focus, and poor commitment are all common causes of the lack of self-discipline. Every step in the P2LR process is designed to improve self-discipline.
Physical Disability: No Arms or Legs	Read the stories of Nick Vujicic and Kyle Maynard below.
Pessimistic Friends and Family	Setting and achieving goals are harder to do when you associate with friends and family that are constantly trying to get you to relapse. It is not a secret in my profession that any time a person in a family or social system tries to change, members of the system will try to keep that person the same. Ironically, this is even true when a person who, after years of addiction, stops drinking. At the time of quitting, the spouse who has begged this person to stop and who has tolerated all kinds of insanity, will oftentimes become irate and subconsciously say and do things that are uncharacteristic and even designed

Table 13

Common Barriers	What IT Is and What You Can Do About IT
Pessimistic Friends and Family (continued)	to trigger the drinking behavior. The point is, for a time at least, you may need to avoid family and friends who try to either consciously or subconsciously undermine your efforts to change.
Negative Environmental Influences Like Bars and Television	The only way to eliminate temptation is to give in to it. And sometimes it is easier to avoid than it is to resist temptation. If you are trying to overcome drinking, it is not a great idea to hang out at a bar. Similarly, if you have a pornography problem, watching sexy movies is not going to help you overcome your addiction.
Lack of Focus	Lack of focus is a barrier for many reasons. At a minimum, if you do not stay focused on where you are going, you will undoubtedly experience several missteps that make the process of change more difficult than it already is. A great way to create focus is to set precise goals that clearly articulate where you are going, how you plan to get there, and when you plan to arrive.
Insufficient Desire	A lack of desire to achieve your goals can be overcome by taking the time to understand motivation and how it can be manufactured through the techniques described in P2LR Step 6. By learning how to focus on the task at hand, nurture motivating thoughts, neutralize negative ones, and reward small steps toward your larger goal, you can create internal desires required to get yourself out of slumps and over the hump before you lose all momentum.

Table 13

Common Barriers	What IT Is and What You Can Do About IT
Inability to Deal with Setbacks	Anyone who sets and starts working toward a goal will experience setbacks. To expect otherwise is completely irrational because it ignores the way life works. In fact, in many cases it is overcoming the setbacks in life that create the greatest sense of accomplishment. Another stumbling block that stops you from growing and succeeding in life is fear. Your fears may include fear of failure, fear of commitment, fear of rejection, fear of public speaking, or even fear of success. Your fears will often tempt you to procrastinate, find excuses, and blame something or someone. When you do bounce back, your ability to recover in the face of adversity will increase. That is, you will become more resilient.
Lack of Confidence	According to Albert Bandura, the father of Social Cognitive Theory, the best predictor of success or failure is the existence or lack of self-efficacy. According to Bandura, self-efficacy is "the belief or confidence in one's capabilities to organize and execute the courses of action required to manage prospective situations." In other words, self-efficacy is a person's belief in his or her ability to succeed in a particular situation. By setting small, achievable goals and, at the same time, learning how to minimize stress and elevate mood when facing difficult or challenging tasks, you can improve your sense of self-efficacy.
Self-Limiting Beliefs	Your irrational beliefs that spawn negative self-talk and irrational stories are also responsible for your doubts, fears, and pessimism. Step 10 will help you learn to

Table 13

Common Barriers	What IT Is and What You Can Do About IT
Self-Limiting Beliefs (continued)	question, challenge, and replace them with empowering beliefs, thoughts, and stories that enable you to change and improve.
	Self-loathing is sometimes used to make "good" excuses to not change. Another self-limiting belief is "That's just the way I am." This belief kills progress and ignores the fact that, with the right plan and motivation, anyone can change.
	"Terminal Uniqueness" is used to describe individuals who have developed what is often referred to as "Learned Helplessness." This is another variant on "That's just the way I am," in that it turns off all motivation because you believe your problem is so special that no one on this planet can ever provide you relief. Before you buy into this state of mental paralysis, please read the stories of Nick and Kyle below. If after reading their stories you say something like, "of course they were very successful, they didn't have arms and legs," you can confidently diagnose yourself as someone who has embraced a state of "Learned Helplessness." Although this is a very difficult condition to overcome, forcing yourself to go through the steps in this book will help you navigate away from this state of hopelessness.
Irrational Thoughts and Behaviors	Thinking or doing things that is inconsistent with or not supportive of your desired vision, goals, and plan of action will consistently undermine your progress and ultimate success. Negative self-talk is an example of irrational thinking. Several steps in the P2LR process are designed to increase congruence between your thoughts and actions, and your plan of action.

Table 13

The good news is that with time and proper planning, you can overcome almost any barrier. This is most obvious in the lives of individuals who have overcome seemingly insurmountable barriers to achieve greatness. Two modern examples of individuals who have accomplished greatness in spite of incredible barriers (both were born without arms or legs), are Nick Vujicic and Kyle Maynard.

Nick Vujicic was born (December 4, 1982) limbless, missing both arms at shoulder level, as well as legs. Where legs should be located, he has a small foot with two toes. In spite of these obvious barriers to any number of goals the average person could easily set and reach, Nick has accomplished more than most people accomplish in a lifetime. He has obtained a double Bachelor's degree, served as President and CEO of a non-profit organization (Life Without Limbs), traveled around the world as a motivational speaker, published several books, and released his own music video.

Kyle Maynard (born March 24, 1986) is a speaker, author, and ESPY award-winning mixed martial arts (MMA) athlete. He has reached these achievements despite being a congenital amputee. Maynard works as a speaker for the Washington Speaker's Bureau, specializing in motivational speeches. He is the author of the memoir No Excuses: The True Story of a Congenital Amputee Who Became a Champion in Wrestling and in Life. He has been featured on talk shows including The Oprah Winfrey Show and Larry King Live.

A documentary film, A Fighting Chance, focuses on his MMA efforts. His amateur debut fight was at Auburn Fight Night at the Auburn Covered Arena in Auburn, Alabama on April 25, 2009. Despite losing his first MMA fight to Bryan Fry on a unanimous 30–27 judges' decision, Maynard eventually received the ESPN Espy Award for Best Athlete With A Disability in 2004. He has modeled for clothing retailer Abercrombie & Fitch. Kyle Maynard is also the owner of No Excuses Crossfit gym located in Suwanee, Georgia. On January 15, 2012, Maynard became the first quadruple amputee to climb Mount Kilimanjaro without assistance, by crawling all 19,340 feet.

The lives of Vujicic and Maynard are proof that, with the right approach and attitude, any barrier can be overcome. This is not to say that everything is possible. Obviously, everyone has real limitations. For example, I will never be the quarterback of the Atlanta Falcons unless I buy the team. I can, however, write and publish several books in spite of the fact that I struggled in junior high and high school because of a learning disability.

How "Ignorance" About "The Psychology of Change" Can Function as a Barrier

Although many barriers will be placed in front of you by circumstances outside your control, such as what happened to Nick and Kyle, many barriers are self-inflicted by lack of knowledge. This type of barrier can readily be overcome by dipping into the vast pool of knowledge that is now available about what does and does not work in the realm of self-improvement. A case in point is the information that was recently published by the Persuasive Technology Lab at Stanford. This prestigious group published a paper on the "Top 10 Mistakes in Behavior Change." I believe that Stanford's findings serve as a good example of the barriers caused by being uninformed can present to a person who earnestly wants to change. Accordingly, I strongly recommend that you consider how to avoid these mistakes as you develop your plan of action in the next step.

1. Relying strictly on willpower for long-term change. The P2LR process addresses this mistake by helping you change the way you see yourself. If you start visualizing yourself doing the things you want to do, you will need considerably less willpower to do it. It will become your passion and purpose. Imagine willpower is like stretching a rubber band as far as you can and holding it there for as long as you can. Eventually, because of the stress, you are going to tire and let go, and the rubber band will snap back to the way it was. If you begin to see yourself as the kind of person who does the kinds of things you want to do, you will naturally return to this new vision of yourself when you are under pressure.

2. Attempting big leaps instead of baby steps. As you will see in the next step, the secret to reaching bigger goals is to set smaller, measurable steps that are approximations of the primary goal. In other words, taking tiny bites is

always the best way to eat an elephant. It allows you to experience small successes, one after another.

3. Ignoring how often environment shapes behaviors. You can avoid this mistake by realizing that you can change your life by changing your context. Marketers understand this and always strive to make the desired behavior (purchasing their product), the easy, fun, and popular behavior. If you make your plan seem fun and easy, it will no doubt be more motivational on those days that you struggle to remember why you are trying to change.

4. Trying to stop old behaviors instead of creating new ones. The point here is to focus on action, not avoidance. In the case of the P2LR process, the focus is on identifying, anticipating, and replacing irrational beliefs, thoughts, and actions that can serve as triggers and barriers to success. The P2LR process will help you replace these old behaviors with new, more positive ones in many different ways.

5. Blaming failures on lack of motivation. Again, it is hard to be motivated to do something that is very different and much harder than what you are accustomed to doing. If you make the behavior fun and easier to do, you will be more likely to maintain your motivation.

6. Underestimating the power of triggers. It is rare that a behavior ever happens without a trigger. Keep track of what you are doing; look for patterns. Find and consciously switch triggers for good behaviors to eliminate the ones that cause you problems.

7. Believing that information leads to action. Humans are not this rational. If this was the case, nurses would not smoke, financially strapped people would not play the lottery, and heart attack sufferers would avoid fatty foods and would exercise on a regular basis.

8. Focusing on abstract goals more than concrete behaviors. Goals to be precise. Goals need to be specific. Generally speaking, a concrete goal is something you can do, now.

9. Seeking to change a behavior forever, not for a short time. Without a doubt, a fixed period of behavior works better than "for time and all eternity."

10. Assuming that behavior change is difficult. Behavior change is not so hard when you have the right process. Simply put, the P2LR process works, if understood and applied correctly. Behavior change is usually the easy part once you have a goal that is aligned with your self-image. This is because your self-image will dictate where you must go to be OK, hence the reason I have placed so much emphasis on getting your self-image right before setting goals.

Taken together, the information provided here regarding triggers and barriers is designed to help you complete the two important action steps: 1) identify, anticipate, and plan to rationally respond to irrational triggers, and 2) identify, break down, anticipate, and plan to overcome barriers that may prevent you from achieving your goals.

Ideas for Implementing This Step & Mastering This Competency

Use the following steps and guides to develop a plan that will help you anticipate and respond rationally to your triggers, and overcome your barriers to becoming your highest and best self. Use the information about triggers and barriers provided above to support you in this efforts.

1. Use the "Trigger Identification and Response Guide" to begin identifying and planning how you will respond to irrational triggers. In column 1, list all the people, places, and things that, when you think about or encounter them, cause you to have the urge to think or do things that are incongruent with your vision and goals. In column 2, record the things that are incongruent with your vision and goals that correspond to each trigger you listed in column 1. Finally, in column 3, list the things you can think or do "INSTEAD OF" those things you listed in column 2. These "INSTEAD OFs" should be consistent with, and in support of, the actions you plan to take toward your vision and goals.

TRIGGER IDENTIFICATION AND
RESPONSE GUIDE

Irrational triggers that cause me to think or do things that are incongruent with my vision and goals	What have I typically thought and/or done in response to the triggers in column 1 that is inconsistent with my vision and goals?	What can I think and/or do in response to the triggers in column 1 that will be consistent with, and in support of, the actions I plan to take toward my vision and goals?

Table 14

2. Use the "Barrier Identification and Response Guide" to begin identifying and planning how you will overcome barriers to your vision, goals, and plan of action. In column 1, list all the thoughts, emotions, actions, people, places, and things that may undermine your ability to realize your vision and achieve your goals. In column 2, describe what you need to think and do to overcome each barrier you listed in column 1.

BARRIER IDENTIFICATION
AND RESPONSE GUIDE

What barriers may prevent me from realizing my vision and achieving my goals?	What can I think or do to overcome the barriers I listed in column 1?

Table 15

3. Use the "RPVS Trigger and Barrier Response Planner" to begin identifying and planning how you will overcome barriers to each element in your Rational Personal Vision Statement. In column 1, list all your RPVS cue words. In column 2, list the triggers and barriers that you anticipate in connection with each element listed in column 1. Finally, in column 3, describe what you will do to deal with each trigger and overcome each barrier listed in Column 1.

RPVS TRIGGER AND BARRIER RESPONSE PLANNER

RPVS Cue Word	Triggers and Barriers that I anticipate in connection with each RPVS element listed in column 1.	What will I think and do to deal with each trigger and overcome the barriers?
CUE 1		
CUE 2		
CUE 3		
CUE 4		
CUE 5		
CUE 6		
CUE 7		
CUE 8		
CUE 9		
CUE 10		

Table 16

MY PLAN FOR P2LR STEP 7

What are the barriers to achieving my goals?

P2LR STEP 8
Create a Plan of Action

Step 8 will help you develop a daily action plan to achieve each of your goals. This plan will consist of a number of clearly defined steps that you will take to achieve each goal. Once you complete your plan of action, you can begin working toward your goals with confidence that you know what it takes to reach your objective.

One of the wise adages that I learned early on when I was an Associate Director of the Public Health Department in Phoenix, AZ, was "If you fail to plan, you plan to fail." Because I did not want to fail, I put a considerable amount of time into planning. Once the plan was in place, I could move forward with confidence that we could eventually turn our goals into a reality. I was also confident that the plan would prevent us from overlooking details; remind my staff and me of our priorities; help us understand what we should and should not do; help us be more efficient, by saving time, money, and energy; and help me hold myself and others accountable to make sure that we did what needed to be done to achieve our goals.

Just as I would not have been successful in managing staff and programs in a large health department without a plan of action, it is very unlikely that you will be successful in achieving a goal without a well-designed plan of action. In effect, your action plan will help you turn your goals (your vision and dreams) into a reality. If you follow the outline here, your plan will specify what you need to do, when you need to do it, and how often. It will also lay out the small, measurable, time-specific steps that you must take to achieve both smaller objectives and the larger goal.

Specifically, each action step in your plan should include the following information: what actions will occur; when you will take each action; how long you will take each action, and what resources (i.e., money, support, equipment) you will need to carry out each action. You should also have some criteria that assure that the steps within the plan and, the plan itself, are rational.

Rational steps and action plans are those that are 1) Congruent: they are consistent with your RPVS elements and the goals linked to each element; 2) Complete: they include all the steps required to do everything that is needed to be done to achieve each goal; 3) Visible: your plan should be available and easy to access. It is not something you can lock in your file drawers and forget about; 4) Clear: although an action plan is always a work in progress, the steps in the plan need to clearly specify what you plan to do, when you will do it, where you will do it, and how often it will be done; 5) Doable: the plan is not overly ambitious. You are confident that you can carry out each step as planned; 6) Effective: your planned actions should actually produce the results you expect them to produce; and 7) Flexible: make sure you build in some contingencies because the best laid plans can be thwarted by unexpected events. Another way of saying this is that you should hope for the best and plan for the worst.

Finally, as will be discussed at length in the last P2LR step, it is important to keep track of what (and how well) you have done. Always keep track of what you have actually accomplished. Ask youself the following questions:

- Am I doing what I planned to do?

- Am I doing it well?

- Is what I am doing advancing me toward my goal?

Ideas for Implementing This Step & Mastering This Competency

Use the "P2LR Action Planner" to develop a realistic plan that will provide you with the steps you will take to achieve your goals and realize your vision. Do this by recording all of the RPVS elements in column 1 and the goal(s) for each element in column 2. In column 3, record the possible barriers to achieving each goal and realizing each vision element. In column 4, list the specific action steps you will take to reach your goals and realize your vision. The action steps should be specific, realistic, measurable, and effective.

P2LR ACTION PLANNER

RPVS Elements	Goals	Barriers	Action Steps

Table 17

MY PLAN FOR P2LR STEP 8

A) What will I need to think to overcome the barriers and achieve these goals?

B) What will I need to do to overcome the barriers and achieve these goals?

P2LR STEP 9
Mentally Program and Internalize Your Plan of Action

Step 9 explains how to use a type of self-hypnosis and imagination to form mental images from your focused thoughts. W. Clement Stone stated, "Whatever the mind of man can conceive and believe, it can achieve." Every creative thing you have ever done begins in your mind as a function of your creative imagination.

As with every book I have written, study I have done, and synthetic learning tool I have developed, the starting point for this book was in my imagination. I began the process by forming concepts, messages, ideas, and images in my creative imagination before I put a single word on paper. And when I did start the arduos task of writing these ideas down, one of the first quotes I came across was from Albert Einstein: " I am enough of an artist to draw freely upon my imagination. Imagination is more important than knowledge. Knowledge is limited. Imagination encircles the world." This quote reinforces my belief in the importance of imagination.

A necessary first step in the psychology of change or in any creative process, including what goes into the process of making personal or interpersonal changes, is imagination. This means that in order for you to become more rational in your life, you must first imagine it. If you cannot imagine it in your mind, you cannot create it in reality. This is true with the way you think about yourself (your self-perception), as well as rational thoughts and actions.

Self-Hypnosis, Visualization, Mental Imaging, and Rehearsal are synthetic learning techniques that rely on your creative imagination to help you improve the rationality and congruence between your self-perception, thoughts, and actions. This step guides you in how to use these techniques to increase your commitment and intensity toward improving your skills, achieving your goals, and realizing your vision.

To use your imagination effectively you must first realize it is enormous power to visualize objects, situations, circumstances, responses to impulses, sound, taste, and other sensations. As a reminder of how readily this power can be accessed, simply close your eyes and imagine yourself standing in front of a large audience that is looking at you as you begin to give a speech about the power of imagination. Or, imagine yourself being chased by an angry dog, or wrestling a bear and winning, or being swallowed whole by a whale, or winning the lottery, or being pronounced king or queen of your country, or being asked on a date by the most attractive person you can "imagine," or imagine yourself standing on a tall building in a hurricane force wind, etc. The capacity to imagine is built into every person and is activated at a very young age. It is the ability to think about people, places, and things beyond your present situation. It is a fundamental aspect of the human condition that allows us to transcend our present circumstances and think about the future, remember the past, solve problems in the present, and strategize about how to effectively create and implement new ideas.

Unfortunately, many parents and educational systems do not teach students how to harness or use their imagination in productive ways to consider new possibilities, alternatives, and hypothetical scenarios. Because of this, many individuals go through life without taking advantage of one of the most powerful tools for personal and professional success— the ability to develop imaginative, innovative thinking. Step 9 will help you maximize your imagination in a way that enables you to control it and visualize only what you intentionally decide to visualize and, in turn, change your life in accordance with your will and imagination.

Imagination has many positive applications, but more than often it is not well-developed or controlled. As with the previous steps, this step will help you better control what you allow to enter your mind and how you use this information to increase your rationality.

Although much of what you have done in the previous steps has no doubt engaged your imagination, this step outlines a process and a number of techniques you can use to begin honing and controlling your imagination in more productive ways. When using these techniques, you can increase your internal motivation and intensity toward achieving your goals with things like motivational literature, pictures, images, videos, and music that are in sync with what you are trying to accomplish. For example, by mentally creating, recreating, and focusing on a goal and the steps required to achieve this goal, and then anticipating and focusing on ways of overcoming barriers to this goal, you can acquire and amplify the personal confidence required to make permanent improvments to your self-perception and your ability to think and act rationally.

One thing that is different about the techniques you will learn here is that they are designed to help you focus on and address specific issues in the form of self-directed assignments. These assignments rely on the use of creative imagination to amplify your capacity to benefit from each technique because they allow you to focus on whatever unique need you have at the time. The assignments you can give yourself are only limited by your imagination. They include such things as setting goals; sorting, prioritizing, and solving problems; learning new skills; relaxing and/or remaining calm under pressure; becoming and remaining more confident; making a presentation to any size group; overcoming bad habits and addictions; answering media questions; and improving relationships.

Ideas for Implementing This Step & Mastering This Competency

There are several steps you can follow to increase your abilities in these mental processes:

1. Start at conscious baseline.

2. Give yourself an assignment, with a specific objective and purpose. Set and attain goals; sort, prioritize, and solve problems; learn new skills; relax and/or remain calm under pressure; become and remain confident; make a presentation to any size group; overcome bad habits and addictions; silence your internal critic; internalize your vision and goals; answer media questions; and improve relationships. Focus on one purpose at a time.

3. Based on the assignment you give yourself, write out suggestions to "make to yourself" as you get into your relaxed state. These suggestions should be consistent with your assignment and help you stay in the "present." For example, you should use "I am" instead of "I will be" statements.

4. Create a place in your mind where you will carry out the assignment (e.g., a workshop, practice field, or resort, decompression chamber, Skillnasium).

5. Select a technique that will help you achieve your purpose.

6. Close your eyes and take time to relax (breathe) until you are ready to take on the assignment.

7. Tune inward with the initial focus on a slow relaxed breath, while at the same time imaging that you are going into a deeper state while counting down slowly from 5, 4, 3, 2, to 1.

8. At this point, use all of your senses to work on your assignment using the suggestions you decided upon. Once

again, when making suggestions use "I am" instead of "I will be" statements.

9. End your assignment with the suggestions that will bring positive benefits from this experience.

10. You are going to become alert and come out of this deeply relaxed state after counting to three: 1, 2, and 3.

11. Return to your baseline.

12. Record your progress so you can carry your accomplishments and good memories with you.

The following comments will help you better understand the process outlined above. Specifically, I provide you with some relaxation techniques and some ideas regarding how to "construct" a place in your mind. I also provide you with some visualization and creativity exercises you can use to mentally program and internalize your vision, goals, and plan of action.

Relaxed Body, Relaxed Mind

As you can see from this list of steps, one of the first things you need to do with each technique is to relax. This is because a relaxed body equates with a relaxed mind, which in turn, improves your ability to focus and attend to your self-directed visualization and imagery assignments.

Relaxation techniques typically combine breathing and

focused attention to calm your body and mind. If used correctly, these techniques will help you quiet your inner critic and increase your ability to carry out your self-directed imagery assignments. In addition to amplifying the benefits of mental imagery and rehearsal, learning and applying relaxation techniques can help with a number of stress-related problems. This is documented in the U.S. National Institutes of Health, National Center for Complementary and Alternative Medicine (NCCAM) Clinical Digest, published in December 2012, which reports evidence that relaxation techniques may be an effective intervention for treating a number of stress-related disorders, including anxiety, phobias, and panic disorder; depression; headaches; lung function and asthma; immune function; heart disease and heart symptoms; hypertension; chronic insomnia; and irritable bowel syndrome.

Other reliable sources have reported evidence that relaxation may help mitigate chronic pain, fibromyalgia, premenstrual syndrome, psoriasis, and hyperactivity related to AD(H)D. The point is, investing the time to relax before using any of the following visualization techniques may have a number of benefits beyond helping you improve your rationality related to your self-image, thoughts, and behaviors.

Selecting the Right Relaxation Technique

The right technique, in the present context, is the one that suits your personal liking and helps you relax and calm your mind in preparation for completing your self-directed imagery assignment(s). Based on my experience with clients and students, the most widely studied techniques that have direct application to this step of the P2LR process are deep breathing and progressive muscle relaxation. Other effective techniques include meditation, guided imagery (similar to what is being taught in this step), self-hypnosis, yoga, Tai Chi, massage, and exercise.

The steps you should follow when using Deep Breathing and Progressive Muscle Relaxation as a means of reaching a relaxed state before doing your visualization and imagery exercise are as follows:

Deep Breathing

1. Get in a comfortable position.

2. Close your eyes.

3. Breathe in through your nose and out through your mouth.

> • As you breathe in through your nose, visualize inhaling pure oxygen that is coated with relaxation.

> • As you breathe out through your mouth, exaggerate the exhalation by visualizing blowing out a birthday candle and imagining that you are releasing tension, stress, and strain. The exaggerated exhalation will speed up the relaxation process.

4. Continue breathing in and out until you are able to feel a sense of calm and have quieted most of the distracting thoughts (e.g., your internal critic) that may interfere with your imagery exercise.

5. Begin your visualization exercise.

Progressive Muscle Relaxation

1. Find a comfortable position.

2. Close your eyes.

3. Visualize scanning your body up and down to find an area that is "more" relaxed than most other places on your body.

4. See yourself breathing into that area (in through your nose and out through your mouth) while imagining that your inhalation is causing the "more" relaxed area to increase in diameter and your exhalation is releasing stress.

5. Do this for about 30 seconds.

6. Now visualize yourself scanning your body to find an area that is more tense than the other parts of your body. Once you have identified this area, start breathing in and out. Once again, imagine that your inhalation is relaxing the area that is "more" tense than other areas in your body. Do this for about 30 seconds.

7. Now start tensing and relaxing muscle groups from your feet to your head while breathing in pure oxygen/relaxation and breathing out stress/tension/strain.

• Imagine flexing the muscles in your feet for 5 seconds and then releasing. The tensing of muscles will bring blood to the area where you have flexed and will cause a sense of warmth and relaxation. Continue breathing in and out while continuing to imagine yourself taking in pure oxygen and releasing stress and strain.

> • Now flex your lower legs for 5 seconds, your calf muscles, while repeating the breathing process.

> • Next, go to your upper legs, then buttocks, abdomen, chest and back, hands, arms, shoulders, neck, and then face. Flex each muscle area for 5 seconds and then release while continuing to breathe throughout the entire process. Continue to focus on breathing in pure oxygen and exhaling all the bad things that are causing your body to tense up and feel stress.

8. After go through the muscle groups, you should be prepared to start the imagery exercise. If not, go through the process of tensing and relaxing your muscles again and again until you are feeling calm.

9. Begin the imagery exercise.

Constructing Places in Your Mind

As I mentioned above, it is helpful to construct a "place in your mind" when you are doing your visualization work. Do not worry about how many places you build as it is estimated that humans have about 100 billion brain cells. This figure does not even include support cells, such as glial cells, that help the neurons; these have been calculated to be at least 10 times more numerous than neurons. This is to say you have plenty of real estate to work with.

Furthermore, do not skimp on the quality of the places you build. Your virtual mental budget is only limited by your imagination. Once again, you can increase your commitment and intensity toward achieving your goals with things like motivational literature, pictures, images, videos, and music that are in sync with what you are trying to accomplish. With these directions in mind, I have provided you with a number of examples of "mental places" you can create and exercises you can carry out in these places. The place I recommend that everyone learn is called a "Mental Home Movie Theater."

Mental Home Movie Theater- Create a movie theater in your mind, including seating and a screen, where you will watch yourself play out a script related to something you want to happen a certain way. Write a script and play the part. Focus on the present as if you are the character that you are watching on screen. Visualize a perfect performance until it happens and you are confident you can play the part. Follow these steps:

1. Create your theater (preferably an IMAX);

2. Write a very good, very comprehensive script. (Write a brief Script for each goal/element in your vision; Watch the Script until you believe it; and Record your progress.)

3. Get in a relaxed state (by using the breathing or muscle relaxation techniques described above).

4. Watch yourself play your part in the movie over and over again until you believe you are the character you are watching. Watch yourself reach, and achieve, your goals.

Mental Practice Room or Field- While the "Mental Movie" technique involves watching yourself play a part, this technique involves visualizing yourself practicing some activity, such as giving a speech, hitting a golf ball, calmly discussing a problem with your spouse, asking for a raise at work, eating a healthy diet, responding rationally to your common triggers. Do this by following these basic steps:

1. Get into a relaxed state.

2. Decide on a purpose.

3. Start Practicing.

Problem Room- This technique creates a place in your mind where you can store your small, medium, and large problems. The rules of this technique include the following:

1. Place all problems in this room.

2. Decide how you will determine the size and importance of the problem.

3. Organize your problems by size and importance.

4. Set a regular schedule to visit, review, and/or work on your problems.

5. Record and store successes and failures for future reference.

Problem Cards- This is one of the most effective exercises you can possibly use when you feel overwhelmed. It will help you get all of your problems out of your head and onto paper. Follow these steps to use this technique:

1. Get 3x5 cards.

2. List each of your most pressing problems on a separate card.

3. Keep your cards with you throughout the day. Also carry a pencil or pen with you.

4. Take your cards to a virtual "problem room" 2 times per day. While you are in this room, review your problems

for several minutes.

5. At any time you have a thought about a problem on one of your cards, write it down on the card.

6. When the problem on a card is solved, place the card in a designated drawer in your home.

Happy Place- This technique creates a place in your mind where you can think about all the things that make you happy. You can also think about what you need to do more or less of to increase your happiness. Follow these steps:

1. Ask yourself the following questions to identify some things you can think or do differently to increase your happiness:

> (a) What do I need to think more about to increase my level of happiness?
> (b) What do I need to think less about to increase my level of happiness?
> (c) What do I need to do more of to increase my level of happiness?
> (d) What do I need to do less of to increase my level of happiness?
> (e) Where do I need to spend more time to increase my level of happiness?
> (f) Where do I need to spend less time to increase my level of happiness?
> (g) With whom should I spend more time to

increase my level of happiness?

(h) With whom should I spend less time to increase my level of happiness?

(i) What will prevent me from thinking and doing the things required to increase my level of happiness?

2. Getting into a relaxed state.

3. Go to your happy place.

4. Start visualizing yourself doing more of and less of those things you wrote down in response to the questions listed above.

5. Record your progress in your journal.

Bad Memory/Failure Dungeon- This technique creates a place where you will lock up all bad experiences and memories that cause you emotional pain. This allows you to confine this pain in one place. Follow these rules when practicing this technique:

1. You must schedule and record all visits in your journal.

2. You can only visit one memory at a time.

3. The purpose of each visit is to find some redeeming quality about the memory. If you cannot find one, you cannot visit again until you come up with a redeeming quality that you can attach to the memory at your next visit.

4. You must put the memories back in the dungeon after the visit.

5. Record your progress in your journal.

Worry World- This technique creates a place in the mind for the purpose of scheduling and carrying out your plans to "worry like crazy!" I say crazy, because if you think about it, worrying is a crazy behavior. Why? Because it is not rational because it does not work. In fact, worrying is harmful in that it creates unnecessary stress. That said, if you are a worrier, I strongly recommend this mental game. To play worry world, do the following:

1. Make a written list of all the things you want to worry about.

2. Schedule specific times to worry.

3. Set a time limit.

4. Stop and start worrying on time.

5. Worry as much as you like when you are in Worry World.

6. Do not worry at all when you are not in the World. That is, if you catch yourself worrying outside of Worry World, quickly schedule an appointment and go there. The trick is to be disciplined about never worrying unless you are in your Worry World at the scheduled time.

7. Record what you learn after each session in your journal.

I Don't Understand File - This technique creates a place in your mind where you can file away things that happen to you that you do not understand. Things happen in our lives that we do not plan and we cannot explain. Instead of getting frustrated and wasting countless hours trying to understand "Why" something happens, you can file these things away in a mental "I Don't Understand" folder, file cabinet, and room. If you go through life trying to figure out why something bad happened or why things did not work out, it will cause you to become bitter and stuck in life. Completing this exercise will allow you to move forward until you get the information you need to put these "I Don't Understand" events into a context and perspective that allows you to learn from the events rather than ruminate over them.

Before providing you with the steps to this technique I will tell you a story that has helped me when I do not understand something that has happend in my life. Over the years as I have travelled to different parts of the globe, I have come to realize a universal principle that is taught in the form of stories in every country I have visited. Although the stories differ, the principle is the same. One of my favorite stories can apply when you start working in your "I Don't Understand" room. It is called Hakuna Matata (Hakuna Matata is a Swahili phrase that can be translated literally as "there are no worries"). Although I do not know how much of it is true (and I have "tweaked" it for the purposes of making a specific point), it does make for a great story.

I heard this version of the story when I was on assignment with the World Health Organization (WHO) in Nigeria. My job was to use my skills as research psychologist in helping the Nigerian government set up a "communication surveillance system" (Cole, 2006) around an outbreak of the H1N4 (bird flu) outbreak. This system was designed to get information from villagers across the country about how they perceived the bird flu, what they did with sick chicken, what they did with a dead chicken, etc. While leading a team of researchers, I was responsible for meeting with the chief of a large (250,000 population) Muslim village. Normally this would not have been a problem, except for the fact that there was a civil war going on between Muslims and Christians.

Because of this, a WHO security officer provided me with some very sobering training about how to get in and out of the village safely. He also explained in some detail how I should meet and greet the Chief. When I entered the home of the Chief, I immediately gained an appreciation for the precautions taken by the WHO security officer given that the Chief was surrounded by guards with machine guns. This gave me a rush of adrenaline that helped me to follow protocol to the letter. Fortunately, the Chief turned out to be a very kind, very gracious host. After asking me to sit down for a conversation, I told him my purpose for coming. In his response he used the words, "Hakuna Matata." When he said this, I must have looked shocked because the way he used the phrase was somewhat different than the way it was used in the Disney movie and the Broadway Musical, The Lion King, where the phrase was interpreted to mean, "Don't worry, be happy." Instead of this interpretation, the Chief used the phrase to mean "It's all good," or "Whatever happens to us is for a reason."

To clarify his use of the phrase in this way, the Chief told me a story about his great grandfather, which illustrates my point regarding the "I Don't Understand" file. The Chief said his great grandfather was a king in northern nigeria near the Congo. He said the King had a servant who was very faithful in carrying out his every command. The only problem was that no matter what happened, the servant would often say the words, "Hakuna Matata," meaning "It's all good." Even though this was annoying to the King, he put up with it since the servant was so obedient. That is until one day, the King and a hunting party were out hunting elephants. During this hunt the King's weapon misfired and blew off the end of one of his fingers. When his favored servant noticed the King was writhing in pain, he started trying to comfort him, and in the midst of his attempts to bring some relief to the King, he used the words "Hakuna Matata." This infuriated the King so much that when they got back to the village he had his servant put in a dungeon.

A few months later the King was on another hunting trip near the Congo. During the hunt the King and his hunting party were surrounded by headhunters (aka, Cannibals) and taken back to their village as captives. Not long after the King and his hunting party arrived at the headhunters' village, the cannibals started sacrificing the men in the King's hunting party one by one to their pagan gods. Because he was dressed as royalty, the King was going to be sacrificed last. When he was being prepared for sacrifice, they noticed he was missing one of his fingers and, because it was bad juju to sacrifice anyone to their gods who was not whole, the King was released. As the King was walking through the jungle back to his own village, he kept looking down at his hand where his finger used to be and saying out loud the words, "Hakuna Matata." He realized that his servant was right, it was a good thing that he lost his finger. With this in mind, the first thing the King did when he got back to the village was to go to the dungeon and have his servant released. When the King saw his servant, he started apologizing for putting him in the dungeon. In response, the servant said, "Hakuna Matata." The King, in turn asked, how can you say "it's all good" when you have been in this dungeon for this long time, and when you look so very thin and pale? The servant then said, "My dear King, had you not put me in this dungeon when you did I would have been on the hunting trip with you and I would have been sacrificed because I am whole."

Once again, this story teaches the idea that we can choose to look at everything that happens to us as a "good thing." I know that when I choose to put a positive spin on what initially appears to be a "bad" situation , even though my heart screams otherwise, it has helped me be "more OK" when things in my life were terribly "not OK." It has also helped buy the time I need to gain the perspective required to understand what "I could not understand" in the first place. And, I might add, in many instances the information and perspective I needed to understand things that I simply "couldn't understand" in my youth did not come until years after the unpleasant events took place.

To use the "I Don't Understand" technique, follow these steps:

1. Create a folder, file cabinet, or room in your mind where you will keep all the things that happen to you that you "Don't Understand."

2. Schedule and record all visits to this room in your journal.

3. Only visit when you are in a good mental state.

4. When you visit, do so with the purpose of finding some redeeming quality about the event you "Don't Understand."

5. Similar to the Bad Memory/Failure Dungeon technique, if you cannot gain any insight during the visit, carefully put the mental file back in its place until the next visit.

6. Record your progress in your journal.

Service Station- This technique creates a place where you go to think about and plan ways to serve others. Based on the self-report of individuals who are truly happy and successful, this is one of the most effective techniques for increasing a sense of meaning, positive emotion, purpose, and accomplishment. Follow these steps:

1. Create a mental room decorated with pictures and quotes that remind you of the benefits of serving others. The room should also have reminders of the kinds of service you want to provide and the types of individuals you would like to serve.

2. Visit the room on a regular basis to review your successes and failures in serving others and to make new plans to serve.

3. Record and store successes and failures for future reference in your journal.

The Armory- This is a room that you visit at the beginning of each day. This is where you begin building and implementing your daily resiliency plan. Follow these simple steps:

1. Develop a resiliency plan.

2. Review the steps in your plan.

3. Record progress in your journal.

Good Memory Lane- This technique creates an actual physical place or a place in your mind where you go to think about and dwell on good memories. Follow these physical or mental steps:

1. Create a place or mental room with reminders of good memories. Include pictures, music, and other reminders of good memories.

2. Get relaxed (by using the breathing or muscle relaxation techniques described earlier).

3. Visit the place and relish in all the good memories;

4. Record in your journal all the good things you remembered, along with the good feelings you had when you were there.

MY PLAN FOR P2LR STEP 9

How will I internalize my plan to overcome my barriers, realize my vision, and achieve my goals?

P2LR STEP 10

Observe and Master Your Internal Monologue

Step 10 will help you recognize the power of combining positive thinking with rational thinking. Our conscious mind has a voice. This is evident because as humans, we talk to ourselves inside all of the time—we think. It is how you know what you are thinking and feeling. In light of this well-known fact, many prominent individuals across history have testified that positive thinking is key to living a happy and successful life. Some examples of quotes by famous individuals about the importance of positive thinking are as follows:

> • For as he thinks in his heart, so is he. (Proverbs 23:7)

> • We are shaped by our thoughts; we become what we think. When the mind is pure, joy follows like a shadow that never leaves. (Buddha)

> • Jesus said unto him, If thou canst believe, all things are possible to him that believeth. (Mark 9:23)

> • Our thoughts determine our lives. (Elder Thaddeus of Vitovnica)

> • Mind is the master power that molds and makes, and man is mind, and evermore he takes . . . The tool of thought, and, shaping what he wills

. . . Brings forth a thousand joys, a thousand ills: He thinks in secret, and it comes to pass: Environment is but his looking-glass. (James Allen)

• The World is what we think it is. If we can change our thoughts, we can change the world. (H.M. Tomlinson)

• We become what we think about. (Earl Nightingale)

• Change your thoughts and you can change the world. (Norman Vincent Peale)

• The pessimist sees the difficulty in every opportunity; an optimist sees the opportunity in every difficulty. (Winston Churchill)

• A man is but the product of his thoughts; what he thinks, he becomes. (Mahatma Gandhi)

• Success is a state of mind. If you want success, start thinking of yourself as a success. (Dr. Joyce Brothers)

• Once you replace negative thoughts with positive ones, you'll start having positive results. (Willie Nelson)

• Every thought is a seed. If you plant crab apples, don't count on harvesting Golden Delicious. (Bill Meyer)

• Thoughts Become Things . . . Choose The Good Ones! (Mike Dooley)

• Cynics do not contribute, skeptics do not create, doubters do not achieve. (Gordon B. Hinckley)

Another example of how the choice to think positively or negatively has long been understood as a factor in how things work out in our lives is found in the poem titled "Thinking," by Walter Wintle.

If you think you are beaten, you are,
If you think you dare not, you don't.
If you like to win, but you think you can't,
It is almost certain you won't.

If you think you'll lose, you're lost,
For out in the world we find,
Success begins with a fellow's will.
It's all in the state of mind.

If you think you are outclassed, you are,
You've got to think high to rise,
You've got to be sure of yourself before
You can ever win a prize.

Life's battles don't always go
To the stronger or faster man.
But soon or late the man who wins,
Is the man who thinks he can.

Although it is true that we tend to become what we think about most of the time, behavioral scientists have demonstrated that to successfully achieve a goal requires more than positive thinking. That is, simply engaging in "positive thinking" is an oversimplification of reality. In light of this discovery, it is more accurate to label positive thinking an "additive" to rational thinking. Positive thinking is necessary to success and emotional well-being, but it is not sufficient.

What's more effective than positive thinking is rational thinking. This is because rational thinking consists of beliefs and thoughts that are logical and consistent with known facts and reality. In addition, rational beliefs and thoughts help you feel the way you want to feel, help you achieve your goals and solve your problems, and support a rational self-perspective.

Albert Ellis, the father of Rational Emotive Behavior Therapy (REBT), once said:

> "We tend to formulate our emotions and our ideas in terms of words and sentences. These effectively become our thoughts and emotions. Therefore, if we are basically the things we tell ourselves, any type of personal change requires us to look first at our internal conversations. Do they serve us or undermine us?"

The point made by Ellis that we need to "look at our internal conversations" is the basis for this step of the P2LR process. Based on my experience in helping individuals overcome every kind of problem you can imagine, before you can make and sustain change in your life, you must

understand how to "see" what you think before you can
change your thought patterns. Once you learn to monitor
and see your thoughts you can then do something about
them. In the context of the P2LR process, this means you
can make whatever effort is necessary to ensure that the
thoughts you think and the stories you tell yourself are
aligned with and support your vision, goals, and plan of
action.

Step 10 will help you systematically observe and master
your internal monologues. You will do this by learning
to observe how you think; make a connection between
what you feel at any one time and what you are thinking;
evaluate your thinking in a way that helps you distinguish
between irrational and rational thoughts; discard thoughts
that do not support your Rational Self-Perception (RSP),
goals, and action plan (irrational thoughts); and replace
irrational thoughts with thoughts that are supportive of
your RSP, goals, and action plan.

The techniques introduced here are based on Cognitive
Behavioral Therapy techniques referred to as Cognitive
Restructuring (David Burns, 1980), Thought Virus
Replacement (Donald Lofland, 1998), Irrational Thought
Replacement (Ellis, Harper & Powers, 1975), and Life
Story Restructuring (Cole, 2013). All of these methods
are designed to help identify and replace dysfunctional
thoughts with more adaptive alternatives. Specifically, these
techniques typically involve learning how to systematically
1) monitor thinking, especially during times of distress; 2)

identify thoughts that are antecedents to negative emotions – the identified thoughts are called cognitive distortions, thought viruses, or irrational thoughts; 3) challenge the validity of the identified maladaptive thoughts; and 4) substitute the cognitive distortions with more rational thoughts.

Generally speaking, the "Thoughts, Emotions, (Re) Actions" model illustrates how these techniques and, more specifically, "Irrational Thought Replacement" works. As you can see, in Figure 7, we all have thoughts that influence how we feel—namely, our emotions. The logic illustrated here is that if you think irrationally, you will feel upset and, in turn, act irrationally. To overcome this maladaptive process, these techniques help you place filters on your thoughts. This means you will examine your thoughts and "throw out" the ones that may cause you to act irrationally. Each of the "rational filters" here is a different question that you will ask of your thoughts in an effort to distinguish the reational ones from the irrational ones. Simply put, when you learn to pay careful attention to your thoughts, you will begin to ask yourself whether or not the thoughts are rational. As depicted in Figure 7, you can ask yourself questions like:

- Is this belief or thought logical?
- Is it consistent with known facts and reality?
- Will it help me feel the way I want to feel?
- Does it contribute to a Rational
  Self-Perception (RSP)?

- Will it improve my sense of well-being, happiness, or serenity?
- Will it help me solve my problems?
- Will it help me achieve my goals?

If you answer no to any of these questions, you must discard the thought. Conversely, if you answer yes to all of the questions, the thought or belief is rational and will support you in your efforts to consistently think and live rationally.

Specific examples of irrational beliefs that tend to spawn irrational thinking came out of the work of Albert Ellis. As introduced in Step 7 of the P2LR process, Ellis identified common irrational beliefs that tend to create irrational thoughts like the ones you will be filtering out using this P2LR step (Step 10). To review, Ellis identified 11 common irrational beliefs: 1) It is a dire necessity for me to be loved or approved by almost all others who are significant to me; 2) I must be thoroughly competent, adequate, and achieving, in all important respects in order to be worthwhile; 3) The world must be fair. People must act fairly and considerately, and if they do not, they are bad, wicked, villainous, or incredibly stupid; they should be severely blamed and punished; 4) It is awful and terrible when things are not the way I very much want them to be; 5) There is not much I can do about my anxiety, anger, depression, or unhappiness because my feelings are caused by what happens to me; 6) If something is dangerous or dreadful, I should be constantly and excessively upset about it and should dwell on the possibility of it occurring; 7) It is easier to avoid and to put off facing life's difficulties and responsibilities than face them; 8) I'm quite dependent on others and need someone stronger than myself to rely upon; I can't run my own life; 9) My past history mainly causes my present feelings and behavior; things from my past, which once strongly influenced me, will always strongly influence me; 10) I must become very anxious, angry, or depressed over someone else's problems and disturbances if I care about that person; and 11) There is a right and perfect solution to almost all problems, and it is awful not to find it.

I suggest that you become familiar with these steps as they will be helpful as you begin the process outlined at the end of this step.

Questions Used to Filter Out Irrational Thoughts

1 Is this thought true? Do I have evidence?
2 Does this thought help me feel the way I want to feel?
3 Will this thought help me overcome my problems?
4 Will it help me achieve my goals and realize my vision?

If you answer **no** to any of these questions you should **throw the thought into the trash can!**

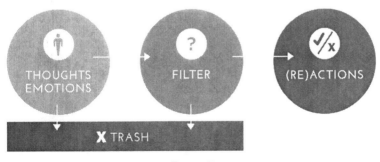

Figure 7

As is explained in Figure 7, the process of repeatedly monitoring, evaluating your thoughts, and discarding those that you deem to be irrational, is not all that is involved in changing maladaptive thoughts to more rational ones. Because you simply cannot stop thinking, when you do discard a thought you must replace it with another thought. This process is depicted in Figure 8. In this figure, you can see that I have provided you with a place to record the thoughts you plan to think "INSTEAD OF" the thoughts you put in the trash can. Once again, these INSTEAD OFs must be rational, in that they are logical, consistent with known facts and reality, help you feel the way you want to feel, contribute to and support your vision, give you a sense of well-being, and help you solve your problems and achieve your goals.

Questions Used to Filter Out Irrational Thoughts

What are the questions you are going to ask yourself to filter out irrational thoughts?

What are you going to think INSTEAD OF the thoughts you put in the trash can?

Figure 8

As is the case with Irrational Thought Replacement, "Cognitive Restructuring" also helps you identify and change out maladaptive thoughts. The main difference is that in the case of Cognitive Restructuring, the maladaptive or irrational thoughts are referred to as "Cognitive Distortions." As was mentioned earlier in Step 7, David Burns, in his popular book, Feeling Good, labels these beliefs that trigger irrational thoughts, urges, and unpleasant emotions, Cognitive Distortions. He explains the most problematic Cognitive Distortions: 1) All or Nothing Thinking - thinking in black and white when many legitimate alternatives exist; 2) Over-Generalization - pretending that everything can be judged by a single occurrence or person. Trying to "tar everything with the same brush;" 3) Mental Filter - seeing only the bad so you lose your perspective. Not widening your focus; 4) Disqualifying the Positive - As it says, this is the way the mind justifies inner-philosophies that make you unhappy; 5) Jumping to Conclusions (a) Mind Reader Error - assuming people think a certain thing when you have no evidence for that, (b) Fortune-Telling Error - assuming that a certain thing will happen when you have no evidence for that; 6) Magnification or Minimalization - blowing things out of proportion or minimalizing the good aspects in yourself or a situation; 7) Emotional Reasoning - taking things personally when they were not meant that way; 8) Should Statement - feeling things should be a certain way that you think best and letting it get to you when they are not; 9) Labeling or Mislabeling - labeling yourself or someone else, rather than seeing them for the whole person they are; and 10) Personalization - thinking that things turn bad because you yourself are bad. I highly recommend this book because it helps you better recognize irrational thoughts so that you can turn them into rational ones.

Thought Virus Replacement

Another technique that illustrates the process of systematically changing irrational thoughts to more rational ones is called "Thought Virus Replacement."As with the other techniques I just described, this step draws upon the principles of Cognitive Behavioral Therapy and Rational Emotive Behavior Therapy. What is different here is my reference to maladaptive thoughts as "Thought Viruses." This term was coined by Donald Lofland in his book Thought Viruses: Powerful Ways to Change Your Thought Patterns and Get What You Want in Life, which I introduced in Step 7, instead of "Irrational Thoughts" or "Cognitive Distortions."

I like to refer to maladaptive thoughts as Thought Viruses for two reasons: 1) I have worked for the U.S. Centers for Disease Control and Prevention for 22 years, and during that time I have learned a lot about pathogens, including viruses, and more importantly, 2) talking about thought viruses is easier to understand and explain than a "cognitive distortion." Even though the term "Cognitive Distortion" sounds more learned, it is simply a label given to thoughts

194

that cause problems. That said, I define a Thought Virus the same way I define irrational thoughts and cognitive distortions. In other words, a Thought Virus is any belief or thought that 1) is not logical; 2) is not consistent with known facts and reality; 3) will not help you feel the way you want to feel; 4) does not contribute to a Rational Self-Perception; 5) will not improve a sense of well-being, happiness, and serenity; 6) will not help you solve your problems; and 7) will not help you achieve your goals.

Once again, as with "Irrational Thought Replacement" and "Cognitive Restructuring," the objective of this "Thought Virus Replacement" technique is to help you learn to systematically identify and replace maladaptive thoughts.

I have provided some examples of the Thought Virus Replacement technique in Figure 9. This figure shows Thought Viruses and "Remedies" to each virus. In this metaphor, the remedies are simply replacement thoughts that you can use to counter Thought Viruses. These new thought remedies are thoughts you will plan to think INSTEAD OF the beliefs and thoughts that are labelled Thought Viruses. Accordingly, they should correspond with and logically replace the Thought Virus you are struggling with.

As you can see in this Figure 9, the process of replacing thought viruses involves listing thoughts in column 1 that make you upset, and listing corresponding thoughts that you plan to think "INSTEAD OF" each thought virus in column 2. Once again, this is exactly the same logic as Cognitive Restructuring and Irrational Thought Replacement where, in both instances, you learn to identify, filter out, and replace maladaptive thoughts with thoughts that are 1) logical; 2) consistent with known facts and reality; 3) help you feel the way you want to feel; 4) contribute to a Rational Self-Perception; 5) improve a sense of well-being, happiness, and serenity; 6) help you solve your problems; and 7) help you achieve your goals.

Irrational Thought Virus	Rational Thought Remedy
*You can begin identifying Thought Viruses by noticing what you are thinking when you are upset. **To be rational, a Thought Remedy must be logical, consistent with known facts and reality, help you feel the way you want to feel, contribute to and support your Rational Personal Vision, give you a sense of wellbeing, and help you solve your problems and achieve your goals.	

Figure 9

When I teach the "Thought Virus Replacement" technique, I typically expand on the Thought Virus metaphor by making the point that irrationality, or irrational thoughts and actions, are the primary cause of emotional upset and instability. This means that anyone or anything in the society or culture that you were socialized in or where you currently live that transmits irrational beliefs or thoughts

196

or actions can be defined, in the language of public health, as an irrational host. Common and powerful hosts and carriers of irrationality in modern society include television, popular movies, parents, teachers, politicians, religious leaders, and so on. These same hosts and carriers also transmit rationality. This is to say that television (more specifically television writers and producers), parents, teachers, politicians, and religious leaders are both hosts and carriers of rationality and irrationality. This means you, the target of their messages, must sort out the difference between those who are feeding you information that will help you or hurt you. Yes, you are responsible for what types of information you consume and believe and act upon.

All said, the solution or cure to irrationality is to decrease irrationality, to increase rationality, or both. At a minimum, the ratio rationality/irrationality (R/IR) needs be between 3:1 and 5:1, which is to say that to be "OK," you must think and behave rationally 3 to 5 times more often than you think and act irrationally. In other words, irrational thoughts and actions tend to inflict much more damage on your emotional well-being than rational thoughts and actions contribute to a healthy emotional state. These ratios are based on assumptions extrapolated from research related to how individuals, couples, and teams/groups respond to negative feedback from their environment. The assumptions are 1) over time, rationality produces positive feedback and irrationality produces negative feedback, and 2) the positivity/negativity ratio (P/N), which is measured by counting the instances of positive feedback versus negative feedback from one's environment, must range from 3:1 (Losada & Heaphy, 2004; Covello, 2009) to 5:1 (Gottman, 1994), to ensure an emotionally healthy state and positive relationships. If you think and do more irrational than rational things, you are not going to be OK. This is why it should be no surprise that those who think about mostly negative things have mostly negative emotions. Conversely, those who tend to think of mostly positive things have mostly positive emotions.

Life Story Restructuring

Another thought replacement technique that I have developed and included here is called "Life Story Restructuring." As with the techniques I just described, this method is designed to help individuals replace irrational ways of thinking with healthier, more rational thoughts and beliefs. The primary difference that makes this approach more practical and, based on my clinical experience, more effective, is the practice of replacing stories instead of specific thoughts.

Focusing on changing stories instead of specific thoughts is more practical because of the shear volume of thoughts that an individual thinks in a single day. It has been estimated that the average person thinks 20,000 to 70,000 thoughts each day. This makes the process of identifying and replacing specific thoughts quite tedious.

To make sense out of all these thoughts, we tend to organize them into stories. These stories are influenced by our experiences with the people we are influenced by during our developmental years—our parents, teachers, and others. These stories help us live in and make sense of the world. They are both conscious and unconscious. And, what is most important here, these stories are both rational and irrational. The good news is that you can become aware of the conscious stories, and the irrational stories can be changed to rational ones.

Because we think thousands of thoughts each day and organize these thoughts into stories that provide context and help us understand the world, it only makes sense that focusing on identifying, evaluating, and replacing irrational stories instead of specific irrational thoughts or beliefs (Cognitive Distortions) is more efficient and, based on my clinical experience, more effective. This is the reason I tend to prefer the Life Story Restructuring method over the other techniques designed to change maladaptive thinking.

The Life Story Restructuring technique is illustrated in Figure 10, which is fittingly labeled the "Life Story Restructuring Guide." As you can see, the process involves recording stories in column 1 that you repeatedly tell yourself that, in turn, cause you to become or remain upset. In column 2, you write a new rational story for each of the irrational stories you list in column 1. More specifically, these new rational stories are what you plan to tell yourself

"INSTEAD OF" the irrational stories recorded in column 1. As with the other techniques described above, to ensure that the new stories are rational, you will evaluate them to ensure that they are 1) logical; 2) consistent with known facts and reality; 3) help you feel the way you want to feel; 4) contribute to a Rational Self-Perception; 5) improve a sense of well-being, happiness, and serenity; 6) help you solve your problems; and 7) help you achieve your goals.

When I teach this approach to changing maladaptive thinking, I often use analogies from my work in Hollywood where I have observed writers changing scripts based on input I provided on different characters. For example, on one occasion I was meeting with a group of writers and a television producer of a popular television series where the lead character had stage IV cancer. During our meeting, the writers and producer made the point that they had a disagreement on how the character would die. The writers wanted this character to model a more dignified dying process while the executive producer wanted her to "go out in flames" as she put it, i.e., live out her last days with reckless abandonment. They asked me what the implications would be in both scenarios. Based on my input they carried on a lively conversation, made some decisions about how the story should play out, and revised the script accordingly. After I left the studio they finalized the script and handed it off to the actress; she rehearsed until she internalized her part, and then she played the part.

All of this serves as great metaphor for Life Story Restructuring and the overall P2LR process, which is designed to help you create a new persona (your Rational Self-Perception), write a script or life story that reflects the "new character" represented by your persona, rehearse and internalize the new script, and live a life that is rational and consistent with your goals and vision of yourself and your future. In other words, the P2LR process taken together with Life Script Restructuring is designed to help you, the producer of your life, write a script, rehearse it until it is believable, and then play the part.

> It's like everyone tells a story about themselves inside their own head. Always. All the time. That story makes you what you are. We build ourselves out of that story.

-Patrick Rothfuss, in the Name of the Wind

To summarize, the techniques discussed in this step (Step 10) are designed to help you systematically increase your awareness of what you are thinking and how your thinking impacts your emotions and overall rationality. All of these approaches are designed to help identify and replace dysfunctional thoughts with more adaptive alternatives. Furthermore, all of these techniques involve (as I outlined at the beginning of this step) learning how to systematically 1) monitor thinking, especially during times of distress; 2) identify thoughts that are antecedents to negative emotions – the identified thoughts are called cognitive distortions, thought viruses, or irrational thoughts; 3) challenge the validity of the identified maladaptive thoughts; and 4) substitute the cognitive distortions with more rational thoughts.

Since the undergirding principles for each of these techniques are virtually the same, I could have used the "Cognitive Distortions" put forward by David Burns in his book Feeling Good, given that Thought Viruses, Irrational Thoughts, and Cognitive Distortions are all the same thing and are dealt with the same way in both Cognitive Restructuring and Thought Virus Replacement exercises. To illustrate how the different labels mean the same thing, I have provided a diagram (see Figure 10) that places Thought Viruses, Cognitive Distortions, Irrational Thoughts, and Irrational Life Stories on the left side of the diagram under the label "Maladaptive Thoughts," and Thought Remedies, Replacement Thoughts, Rational Thoughts, and Rational Life Stories underneath the heading entitled "More Adaptive Thoughts."

Labels use to represent Maladaptive Thoughts	Labels use to represent More Adaptive Thoughts
Cognitive Distortions	Replacement Thoughts
Irrational Thoughts	Rational Thoughts
Irrational Life Story	Rational Life Story

*You can begin identifying Thought Viruses by noticing what you are thinking when you are upset.
**To be rational, a Thought Remedy must be logical, consistent with known facts and reality, help you feel the way you want to feel, contribute to and support your Rational Personal Vision, give you a sense of wellbeing, and help you solve your problems and achieve your goals.

Figure 10

Finally, before you do what is required to implement this step (Step 10), it is helpful to understand the logic that supports the need for consistently monitoring and mastering your internal monologue to ensure alignment between what you are thinking and your vision, goals, actions, and thoughts. This logic is shown here in Figure 11. This figure is based on the Stress Response Cycle introduced (SRC) in Section III. This version of the SRC illustrates that all problems (anything that causes stress) are caused by Irrational Beliefs, Irrational Thoughts, Irrational Actions, and Life Events, i.e., difficult people, places, and things that create discrepancies between expectations and reality (Cole, 1985), and the total number of problems a person experiences is directly proportionate to his or her level of stress. This means that anything that can be done to eliminate irrational beliefs, thoughts, and actions will, in turn, reduce the amount of distress experienced by the individual who can increase his or her rationality. As can also be seen in this diagram, the purpose of this P2LR Step is to help you eliminate your irrational beliefs, thoughts, and actions that are causing emotional distress. This doesn't mean you won't experience stress. We all have difficult stress-inducing life events (Cole, 1985) that are unavoidable. What it does mean is that through the techniques presented in this step you can increase your "mindfulness" by decreasing the problems and distress caused by your irrational beliefs, thoughts, and behaviors.

STRESS RESPONSE CYCLE

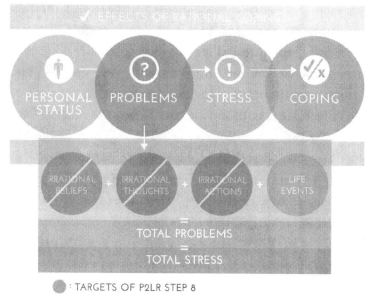

⬤ : TARGETS OF P2LR STEP 8

Figure 11

Ideas for Implementing This Step & Mastering This Competency

You can implement this step by using one of the two guides that follows. I suggest that you start with the "Thought Observation and Restructuring Guide" to help you see the connection between your emotions, beliefs, and thoughts. I have divided this Guide into two parts. Part 1 helps you track and monitor your thoughts to distinguish between rational and irrational thoughts. Part 2 helps you replace irrational thoughts. After learning how to use this process, I recommend that you move on to and make a habit of using the "Life Story Restructuring Guide," as it is easier to integrate into your day-to-day life.

The Thought Observation and Restructuring Guide

Thought Observation and Restructuring Guide: Part 1

The way you think and the things you do have an impact on your emotions and sense of well-being. If you hold on to irrational beliefs (see Reference 2, which immediately follows) and/or you think negative thoughts, you will feel negative emotions (see Reference 1, which immediately follows). Consequently, to decrease your negative emotions you can replace irrational beliefs and thoughts that cause unpleasant feelings with thoughts that produce more positive emotions.

The "Thought Observation and Restructuring Guide" is designed to help you identify and replace thoughts and thought patterns that cause unpleasant emotions. Part 1 of this guide will help you monitor and evaluate your thoughts as they relate to your negative emotions. Tables A and B below are designed to help you organize yourself as you go through this thought-restructuring process.

To start the process, complete the following steps: 1) monitor your emotions throughout the day; 2) record negative emotions in column 1, Table A; 3) in column 2, record the time and context of what is going on at the time you notice the negative emotions; 4) determine which thoughts are associated with the emotions listed in column 1; 5) record negative thoughts in column 3; 6) evaluate each thought recorded in column 3 by answering the questions in column 4. Referring to the information you gathered using the "Hassle Tracker" (introduced in Step 1) should be helpful here.

Use the "Cognitive Filtering & Refinement" exercise to practice filtering out and replacing thoughts that are causing the negative emotions you record in column 1 of the "Thought Observation Guide" and ensure that your thoughts are consistent with your Rational Personal Vision Statement and goals.

After completing Table A (in Part 1), go on to Table B (in Part 2) where you will record replacement thoughts for the irrational and distorted thoughts you have recorded in Column 3, Table A.

TABLE A - Thought Record

Negative Emotions (Examples of Negative Emotions are Listed below in Reference 1)	
Day/Time/Event (When did I notice the negative emotion and what was going on around the same time?)	
Related Thoughts (The Thoughts I am thinking when I am Upset)	

TABLE A - Thought Record (continued)

Evaluate My Thoughts (These are Rules that will help me Referee my Thoughts)	
Is it Rational? (See Reference 2)	Is it Distorted? (See Reference 3)

Reference 1

Common Negative Emotions

Embarrassed, guilty, angry, sad, incompetent, afraid, anxious, hopeless, unhappy, disappointed, pessimistic, frustrated, regretful, lonely, inferior, panicky, worthless

Reference 2

Irrational Thinking

To sum up our definition used in Step 10, irrational thinking includes thoughts that are 1) not based on fact, 2) do not help you feel the way you want to feel, and 3) do not help you achieve your goals. To review Albert Ellis (a behavioral scientist) for purposes of this exercise, the most common irrational thoughts among Americans are as follows:

1) It is a dire necessity for me to be loved or approved by almost all others who are significant to me.

2) I must be thoroughly competent, adequate, and achieving, in all important respects in order to be worthwhile.

3) The world must be fair. People must act fairly and considerately, and if they do not, they are bad, wicked, villainous, or incredibly stupid; they should be severely blamed and punished.

4) It is awful and terrible when things are not the way I very much want them to be.

5) There is not much I can do about my anxiety, anger, depression, or unhappiness because my feelings are caused by what happens to me.

 6) If something is dangerous or dreadful, I should be constantly and excessively upset about it and should dwell on the possibility of it occurring.

7) It is easier to avoid and to put off facing life's difficulties and responsibilities than face them.

8) I'm quite dependent on others and need someone stronger than myself to rely upon; I can't run my own life.

9) My past history mainly causes my present feelings and behavior; things from my past, which once strongly influenced me, will always strongly influence me.

10) I must become very anxious, angry, or depressed over someone else's problems and disturbances if I care about that person.

11) There is a right and perfect solution to almost all problems, and it is awful not to find it.

Reference 3

Cognitive Distortions

Irrational thoughts are sometimes labeled as cognitive distortions. Cognitive distortions are patterns of thinking that produce illogical thoughts that oftentimes produce negative emotions. Once again we will review the 10 most common cognitive distortions (David Burns, Feeling Good):

1) All or Nothing Thinking - thinking in black and white when many legitimate alternatives exist.

2) Over-Generalization - pretending that everything can be judged by a single occurrence or person. Trying to "tar everything with the same brush."

3) Mental Filter - seeing only the bad so you lose your perspective. Not widening your focus.

4) Disqualifying the Positive - As it says, this is the way the mind justifies inner-philosophies that make you unhappy.

5) Jumping to Conclusions (a) Mind Reader Error - assuming people think a certain thing when you have no evidence for that, (b) Fortune-Telling Error - assuming that a certain thing will happen when you have no evidence for that.

6) Magnification or Minimalization - blowing things out

of proportion or minimalizing the good aspects in yourself or a situation.

7) Emotional Reasoning - taking things personally when they were not meant that way.

8) Should Statement - feeling things should be a certain way that you think best and letting it get to you when they are not.

9) Labeling or Mislabeling - labeling yourself or someone else, rather than seeing them for the whole person they are.

10) Personalization - thinking that things turn bad because you yourself are bad.

The Thought Observation and Restructuring Guide

Thought Observation and Restructuring Guide: Part 2

The second part of this guide is designed to systematically help you replace irrational and distorted thoughts and thought patterns. Place all of the distorted and irrational thoughts you recorded in Table A, in column 1 of Table B. 1) Decide on new thoughts you can use to counter the irrational thoughts listed in column 1; 2) list your replacement thoughts in column 2; and 3) in columns 3 and 4, respectively, develop a practice schedule for overcoming your irrational thinking. Share your progress with your therapist, if applicable.

TABLE B
"Replacement Thought" Practice Schedule

Irrational and/or Distorted Thoughts (Taken from column 3, in Table A)	
Rational Replacement Thoughts	
When and Where I Will Practice New Rational Thinking	
How Often I Will Practice	

The Life Story Restructuring Guide

Use the "Life Story Restructuring Guide" to systematically identify stories that you tell yourself that make you upset. These stories come out of irrational beliefs that undermine your goals and your rational vision of yourself and your future. They limit your potential by dictating what you can and cannot become, do, and get in life. As with the previous exercise, the way you identify these stories is by tracking and documenting what you are telling yourself when you are upset. Usually when you are upset, you are telling yourself a story that causes you to feel bad. This also means that to change your negative emotions you must edit or replace the stories that upset you with rational stories. By rational stories, I mean stories that you tell yourself that are 1) logical and consistent with known facts and reality—based on truth; 2) produce desired emotions; 3) help overcome current and future problems; 4) encourage serenity, personal growth, development, and happiness; 5) encourage learning from the past, preparing for the future, and living in the present; 6) support personal and interpersonal goals; and 7) support an optimistic view of one's self and future. Conversely, a story is irrational if it 1) is not logical and/or there is no evidence to support it as true; 2) does not help you feel the way you want to feel; 3) does not help you overcome your problems; 4) is destructive to yourself or others; and/or 5) undermines your goals.

Before you begin, you should recall Section III, which introduces Self-Sabotage. Remember, any time you attempt to change long-held beliefs, you will experience resistance. At times the negative stories you have consistently told yourself over time will re-enter your mind and cause you to feel sad and upset, even when you are attempting to feel happy and fulfilled. This incongruence will initially cause you to feel "Change-Based Cognitive Dissonance." As you will recall from what was discussed in Step 7, this type of dissonance occurs any time you think and do things that are different than things you have thought and done in the past, such as starting to exercise when you have not exercised in the past, or moving from a country where you drive on the right side of the road to a country where you drive on the left side. When this dissonance happens simply remind yourself that this is normal and healthy and that with time and persistence it will subside.

An important thing to remember here, as with other maladaptive thought-restructuring techniques, is that what you say to yourself (think) determines how you feel. And, your thoughts and feelings have an impact on your actions.

If the stories you tell yourself are upsetting, you will be upset whenever you think about these stories. If you tell yourself upsetting stories over and over again, you will undoubtedly experience a multitude of upsetting emotions like fear, discouragement, or sadness. Fortunately, because you have control over the thoughts and personal life stories you think about, you can replace or modify thoughts and the stories you tell yourself in a way that changes the way you feel. This requires a careful analysis of what is upsetting you and reframing the thoughts that are upsetting into more rational thoughts and stories.

The process for completing the "Life Story Restructuring Guide" is somewhat self-explanatory. It involves observing your emotions throughout the day until you notice that you are upset. At that point, record the story or stories you are telling yourself in column 1 of the guide. Once you have documented an irrational story in column 1, write a new script or story in column 2 that is rational. To review our definition, a rational story is 1) logical; 2) consistent with known facts and reality; 3) helps you feel the way you want to feel; 4) contributes to a Rational Self-Perception; 5) improves a sense of well-being, happiness, and serenity; 6) helps you solve your problems; and 7) helps you achieve your goals. Rehearse the script until you believe it. Finally, any time an old, irrational story crops up, replace it with the new rational story. Do this until the old story is no longer a problem.

LIFE STORY RESTRUCTURING GUIDE

Old stories You tell yourself that upset you *Irrational stories	New stories You plan to tell yourself to overcome old stories **Rational, replacement stories
* You can begin identifying irrational stories by noticing what you are telling yourself when you are upset. ** To be considered rational, a story must be logical, consistent with known facts and reality, help you feel the way you want to feel, contribute to and support your Rational Personal Vision, give you a sense of well-being, and help you solve your problems and achieve your goals.	

Figure 12

Another exercise you can use to master the skill of aligning your thinking with your vision, goals, and plan of action is illustrated here in the "Talk the Talk" matrix below. Begin using the matrix by writing a single goal in row 1. Then, in column 1, record the stories you typically tell yourself that undermine this particular goal. For each story in column 1, write a new story in column 2 that reframes your old story into a rational story that supports your goal.

The new stories are what you will tell yourself "INSTEAD OF" the stories that undermine your goals. In column 3, you will explain A) "Why" you want the rational stories to come to pass, and B) "What" you plan to think and do differently to make the rational stories come true.

Finally, you will notice that the arrow on this matrix is labelled AT2R (Acknowledge irrational story, and Transition 2 the Rational story), which is designed to remind you of the action you need to take every time you start telling yourself an old story. The logic here is that when stress triggers an irrational story, you will not suddenly invent and start telling yourself a new, more rational story unless you have developed and practiced telling yourself this story in advance of the stressful event. As I am sure you have already noticed, this same logic applies to all of the maladaptive thought restructuring exercises where you learn to anticipate irrational thoughts and stories and prepare yourself to counter them with more adaptive thoughts. What is new here is the AT2R acronym, which is designed to remind you what to do when irrational thoughts and stories crop up. For example, as soon as you notice that you are thinking one of the stories you have recorded in column 1, you will immediately say to yourself "AT2R" to remind yourself to transition to a corresponding rational story in column 2. Obviously, this takes practice using the tools provided in P2LR Step 9.

TALKING THE TALK

Record one of your goals here:		
What are the stories you tell yourself that undermine your goals?	Reframe your old story into rational stories that support your goals. These are stories that you will tell yourself **instead of** the stories that undermine your goals.	Why do you want the rational stories to come to pass? What will you need to think and do differently to make the rational stories come true?
Irrational Story #1	• Acknowledge Irrational Story • Transition to Rational Story	
Irrational Story #2		
Irrational Story #3		

Table 18

MY PLAN FOR P2LR STEP 10

What will I do to keep my thoughts in support of, and aligned with, my overall plan?

P2LR STEP 11
Plan to Cope Rationally

Step 11 revisits some of the rational coping techniques introduced in Section III. As is illustrated in the Stress Response Cycle (SRC) below, all of us experience problems, which can lead to emotional pain called stress. In fact, stress is a normal response to anything that makes us feel keyed up, threatened, or upset (Cole, Tucker & Friedman, 1990; Cole, Tucker & Friedman, 1986; Cole, 1985). In other words, when people, places, or things are not the way we want them to be, we experience stress.

Stress can be a good thing when it motivates you to escape from a dangerous situation or when it helps you stay energetic and alert. However, when it causes chronic psychological or physical pain, it is a message to our brain that something is wrong. This message motivates us to think or do something to get rid of the pain.

To review, the things we think and do to get rid of this pain are called coping responses. Because stress is a form of pain and, because we are programmed from birth to react to pain, when we experience stress caused by a problem we begin coping in an effort to reduce the pain. Think back to the example of touching a hot stove. An infant's coping response to pain is to cry out. However, as we get older, our coping responses become more sophisticated to remove the pain. As adults, if we touch a hot stove, we know to quickly pull back in response to the pain.

ADDING A COPING PLAN TO THE STRESS RESPONSE CYCLE

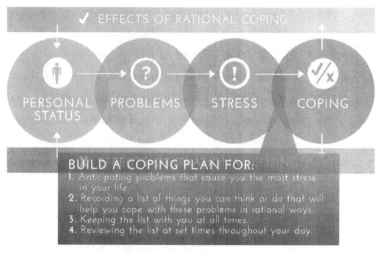

Figure 13

Some very important truths about coping are illustrated in the "SRC Coping Window" in Table 19 (which was introduced in Section III). Again, we should review that there are two broad types of coping—rational and irrational. (These terms are interchangeable with other descriptors, such as healthy and unhealthy, wise and unwise, right(eous) and unright(eous), effective and ineffective).

As can be seen in this diagram, both types of coping are the same with one exception. Rational coping makes an individual stronger whereas irrational coping makes an individual weaker. This is one of the keys to understanding why two similar individuals who have the same problem end up in very different places. To review the example in Section III, a person who drinks alcohol to deal with stress will have a much different outcome from a person who engages in aerobic exercise (running or cycling) to relieve the stress-induced pain (Page & Cole, 1991; Cole, Tucker & Friedman, 1990). Both individuals will get some relief; however, exercising is a much more healthy (both physically and emotionally) coping strategy. Review the "SRC Coping Window" table that was introduced in Section III as you consider ways to cope rationally.

SRC COPING WINDOW

Characteristics of Rational, Healthy, Wise, Effective, Right(eous) COPING RESPONSES	Characteristics of Irrational, Unhealthy, Unwise, Ineffective, Unright(eous) COPING RESPONSES
A way of thinking or acting in response to stress	A way of thinking or acting in response to stress
Relieves pain caused by stress	Relieves pain caused by stress
Requires mental or physical effort	Requires mental or physical effort
Requires varying degrees of discipline	Requires minimal if any discipline. Referred to as "the Path of Least Resistance," or the "Softer, Easier Path"

Table 19

219

SRC COPING WINDOW (continued)

Characteristics of Rational, Healthy, Wise, Effective, Right(eous) COPING RESPONSES	Characteristics of Irrational, Unhealthy, Unwise, Ineffective, Unright(eous) COPING RESPONSES
Oftentimes more difficult in the short term	Often easier in the short term and more difficult in the long term. Referred to as a "quick fix"
Requires internal locus of control	Rooted in external locus of control
Helps achieve rational goals	Prevents achievement of rational goals
Is moral, ethical, and legal	In some instances, is immoral, unethical, or illegal
Requires personal resilience that is commensurate with the amount the magnitude of the adversity encountered	Does not require resilience
Makes an individual stronger, healthier, more independent, wiser, more effective	Makes an individual weaker, unhealthy, more dependent, unwise, less effective

Table 19

Ideas for Implementing This Step & Mastering This Competency

Complete and begin implementing the "Coping Plan Matrix." This exercise will help you plan new ways of coping in response to daily stressors. If you do not think about new ways of coping in response to issues you have struggled with in the past, you will not be able to change. You simply cannot change the way you perform under stress unless you have thought about and practiced new ways of coping. This is all to say, "Failing to plan is a way of planning to fail."

TRIGGER IDENTIFICATION AND RESPONSE GUIDE

List the problems that have caused, or that I anticipate will cause, the most stress during my day/week/month.	What do I typically think and do in response to stress induced by the problem listed in column 1?	What I plan to think and/or do differently? (Ideas for replacement thoughts and actions are provided in the Appendices at the end of this section.) These new coping responses should 1) prove to be effective, 2) help me feel the way I want to feel, and 3) help me achieve my goals.

Table 20

After you have completed your new Coping Plan, practice the Anti-Flacting technique. The following diagram explains how to counteract your triggers (which were identified in Step 7) and the negative emotions they produce. Instead of reacting like you have in the past, this process can help you cope in a healthier way. The diagram reminds you to do the following: 1) breathe; 2) tell yourself you are upset; 3) tell yourself this is an opportunity to change and become stronger; and 4) tell yourself of the many things in your coping plan that you will think and do INSTEAD OF the things you have done in the past that did not work. Review this approach daily and practice using it every time you get upset.

ANTI-FLACTING

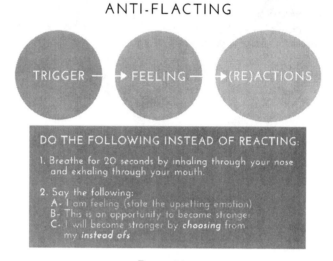

TRIGGER → → FEELING → → (RE)ACTIONS

DO THE FOLLOWING INSTEAD OF REACTING:

1. Breathe for 20 seconds by inhaling through your nose and exhaling through your mouth.

2. Say the following:
A- I am feeling (state the upsetting emotion)
B- This is an opportunity to become stronger
C- I will become stronger by *choosing* from my *instead ofs*

Figure 14

MY PLAN FOR P2LR STEP 11

How will I cope when I am under stress?
That is, what will I do INSTEAD OF those things I typically do when I am under a lot of stress?

P2LR STEP 12
Evaluate Your Progress and Adjust Your Plan of Action

Step 12, the final step in the P2LR process, helps you establish a process for monitoring your performance and progress. This process will help you identify and better understand the "hows" and "whys" behind your failures and successes. This understanding will enable you to overcome your failures and replicate your success over and over again.

Attempting to evaluate your progress can be a frustrating process that is also a waste of time and energy unless you design and implement a clear plan of action in advance (Cole, 1999). To do this requires some understanding of how to set and measure your progress against performance standards (Cole, Pogostin, Westover, Rios & Collier, 1995).

Performance standards are those expectations you have concerning how you want to go about achieving your goals and realizing your vision. When you evaluate your performance, you compare what you want or expect your performance to be (the performance standard) against what you actually think or do. If there is considerable discrepancy between what you want to think and do and what you actually think and do, then you are underperforming.

Poor performance typically results under these four conditions: when you are not fully committed to your goal; when you are not clear about what the goal is; when you do not clearly articulate the steps you need to take to achieve your goal; or when you do not have something (e.g., knowledge, skills, motivation, equipment, or support) that is required to carry out the steps in your plan. With this in mind, you will use the methods described below to 1) evaluate how you are doing by comparing what you have laid out in your goals and plan of action against what you are actually doing, and 2),hold yourself accountable if there is a discrepancy. You must be willing to admit you are not performing as planned and make whatever changes are necessary to your plan or your performance to get back on track.

Ideas for Implementing This Step & Mastering This Competency

The following ideas will help you develop a plan for determining how you are doing and what you need to change to improve your performance. Essentially, this involves asking yourself questions that provide you insight into whether or not you are doing what you plan to think and do to achieve your goals. You may want to routinely ask yourself these specific questions:

- Am I making progress toward my goal?
- What am I doing that is going well and why?
- What am I doing that is not working and why?
- What could I do better with a little tweaking?

- What should I stop doing so I can do other things?
- Where is my time most being wasted?
- What discipline do I most need to implement into my day?
- What drains my energy just to think about doing again?
- What changes do I need to make?

Another set of questions focuses specifically on what you should THINK or DO more or less of to improve. You may want to refer back to the Happiness Algorithm Planner (HAP) you filled out in Section I to answer these questions:

- What do I need to think more about to achieve this goal?
- What do I need to think less about to achieve this goal?
- What do I need to do more of to achieve this goal?
- What do I need to do less of to achieve this goal?
- Where do I need to spend more time?
- Where do I need to spend less time?
- With whom should I spend more time?
- With whom should I spend less time?
- What will prevent me from thinking and doing these things (knowledge, skills, motivation)?
- Who may prevent me from doing these things?

Finally, use the "Evaluation Planning Guide" as a model for developing a system to track and document your progress

(Cole, 1999). In column 1, list the goals you plan to track with this guide. In column 2, record the action steps you plan to carry out to achieve each goal. In column 3, describe how you will know whether or not you can carry out each action step and achieve your goals. Lastly, in column 4, document your successes and failures. When you document failures, record what you plan to think or do differently to get back on track toward your goals.

P2LR EVALUATION PLANNING GUIDE

What Goals Do I Plan to Track?	
What Action Steps Do I Plan to Track?	
How Will I Know if I Carry Out My Action Steps and Achieve My Goals? (My Performance Standards)	
What Will I Think or Do Differently to Overcome My Failures?	

Table 21

MY PLAN FOR P2LR STEP 12

How will I track my progress and make necessary adjustments to ensure my success?

SUMMARY AND CONCLUSIONS

To summarize, the contents of this book represent a serious approach to psychological change, personal and interpersonal development, and recovery. Although there are many approaches to change out there that are helpful, I believe my approach is effective because I offer you a tried and true recipe for personal and interpersonal development and recovery. As I explained in the Introduction, the 12 Steps in the P2LR process are based on principles that have proven universally effective in my clinics and on large populations around the world. I believe these principles have helped, and will continue to help, men, women and children, of different races, from different cultures and religions, around the globe learn to live rational, productive, happy lives.

Turkish Proverb reminds us that change is possible: "No matter how far you have gone on the wrong road, turn back." The point is that all of us make mistakes, and when we realize we have made one, we need to turn our lives in a different direction.

Unfortunately, many individuals do not have the courage or wherewithal to "turn back." At the same time, many who do want to change do not know how to make and sustain the changes required to get back, and stay, on a good path. My point is that the principles, tools, and techniques presented here will help you gain the motivation to change and will provide you with the tools required to become your highest and best self.

Once you do gain the courage, knowledge, skills, and tools required to turn your life around, it is recommended that you get started sooner than later. Once again, I refer Robert Louis Stevenson, who motivates us to make the change today: "No man can run away from weakness. He must either fight it out or perish. And if that be so . . . why not now, and where you stand." Another way I can express this sense of urgency is to ask you the question: "Is it better to start thinking and doing things to increase your happiness sooner, or later?"

Obviously, if your goal is to increase your happiness, it is a good idea to start the process as soon as you have developed a specific, realistic plan that will help you navigate the complexities of permanent change and self-improvement.

The express purpose of the P2LR process is to help you develop a comprehensive plan for change and self-improvement. In other words, the P2LR process shows how "the psychology of change" can help individuals, couples, and families systematically improve themselves and their relationships, and even overcome serious problems such as addictions, by eliminating unhealthy and irrational thoughts and actions and replacing them with attitudes and actions that produce rational living, increased happiness, health, and serenity

Although many people resist the "P" (Planning) in the P2LR process, I have learned, in both a clinical setting and in my international humanitarian efforts, that to make healthy choices and changes, individuals need well-organized, comprehensive information to develop and maintain a truly happy lifestyle. I have also learned that without detailed, specific information for action, the good intentions of most individuals will remain just that—good intentions. With this in mind, I have provided you with very detailed information laid out in a process that is readily understood and applied. I also have referred back to the same core principles and have repeatedly encouraged you to complete, then repeat, the included exercises as a way to reinforce rational thinking and behavior that will lead to lifelong positive changes in your own life and in your relationships.

This is an ongoing process and not a one-time event that results from a powerful or dramatic experience. Gradually, as is depicted in the diagram labeled "Samples of Positive Effects of P2LR Steps on the Stress Response Cycle," using the P2LR steps as prescribed will provide many benefits. Specifically, you will begin to 1) improve your ability to monitor your status and design effective plans to improve emotional well-being; 2) increase your Internal Locus of Control; 3) reduce or eliminate problems caused by irrational thoughts and actions, irrational beliefs, thoughts, and actions; 4) reduce stress caused by irrational thoughts and actions; 5) build resiliency that improves emotional regulation and distress tolerance; and 6) increase rational coping and improve personal well-being. As you persist in applying the 12 steps, the P2LR process will enlarge, deepen, broaden, and amplify your highest aspirations for happiness, health, and a sense of true serenity.

SAMPLES OF POSITIVE EFFECTS OF P2LR STEPS ON THE STRESS RESPONSE CYCLE

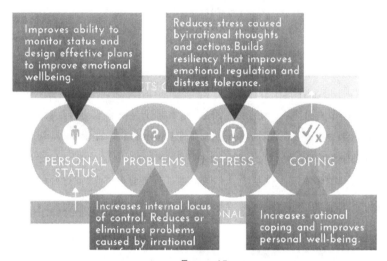

Figure 15

These deep-seeded changes are made possible by following specific steps in the P2LR process. Some of the changes and the corresponding steps that lead to these changes are once again listed for your review:

1) To know how you are doing and whether or not you are making progress, you must monitor how you are doing

(P2LR Steps 1, 10 & 12).

2) You can change your life and your future by creating a new persona—becoming a new character (P2LR Step 4).

3) To change your persona (character), you must become motivated to write a new script (goals and a plan of action) that describes how you will think and act in your new role (P2LR Steps 5-8).

4) You must rehearse the script until you take on the new persona and become the new character (P2LR Step 9).

5) You must think and do what is required to continue playing the new role outlined in your new script and represented by your new persona (P2LR Steps 10-12).

Finally, I return to a quote by Einstein: "Make everything as simple as possible, but not simpler." The last section of the book provides you with some P2LR shortcuts. Once you master the 12-step process described in Section IV, I recommend that you try out the "Quick Start" tools in Section V. These abbreviated routines build on everything that is laid out in the previous sections.

SECTION V
ABBREVIATED PLANNING TOOLS
FOR CHANGE, GROWTH, DEVELOPMENT
& RECOVERY

This section introduces and explains two "Quick Start" tools that you can use once you have become familiar with the 12 P2LR steps. These abbreviated routines build on everything that is laid out in the previous sections. They are easy to learn and apply to any problem you want to overcome, or to any goal you want to set and achieve.

QUICK START 1
Abbreviated P2LR Implementation Plan

Once you have gone through the explanation of each of the 12 P2LR steps outlined in Section IV of the book, you can use this abbreviated version of the steps to develop a specific plan to change or improve yourself. You will notice at the beginning of each step, I have provided you with a question and a place to answer the question. In effect, your response to each question will be your plan for implementing the step.

Taken together, the answers you record across all the steps will be your "Self-Directed Change Plan" as it relates to whatever you are trying to accomplish. The "P2LR Prompt Question" leads to specific questions that directly correspond with each step of the P2LR process:

P2LR Prompt Question

What do I want to change or improve in my life?

1. How will I keep track of how I am doing relative to what I am trying to change or improve?

2. How will I solve problems I encounter when trying to change?

3. What will I do to build and maintain my resilience?

4. How will I need to see myself to change or become the kind of person who consistently accomplishes these things (add elements to my RPVS)?

5. What are my short-, medium-, and long-term goals?

6. What will motivate me to achieve my goals?

7. What are the barriers to achieving my goals?

8. A) What will I need to think to overcome the barriers and achieve these goals?

B) What will I need to do to overcome the barriers and achieve these goals?

9. How will I internalize my plan to overcome my barriers, realize my vision, and achieve my goals?

10. What will I do to keep my thoughts in support of, and aligned with, my plan?

11. How will I cope when I am under stress?

12. How will I track my progress and make necessary adjustments to ensure my success?

P2LR Prompt Question

What do I want to change or improve in my life?

P2LR STEP 1

Monitor Your Personal Status.

How will I keep track of how I am doing relative to what

I am trying to change or improve?

Ideas for Implementation

Knowing how you are doing throughout the day is the first step in the process of intentional change. It allows you to determine such things as whether or not you are making progress, what is working and what is not working, beginning to see what is going on inside and outside yourself when you are OK and, when you are not OK.

To begin this personal observation process 1) decide on how you will record your status (e.g., journal, diary, notebook, computer); 2) check your status three times per day and record your answers to the three questions on the "Life Satisfaction Scale;" 3) every night before you go to sleep, write down three things that went well during the day and why; and 4) use the "Hassle Tracker" to identify what is upsetting you on a consistent basis. Perform each of these status checks for at least seven consecutive days.

LIFE SATISFACTION SCALE

(Terrible) 0 -- 1 -- 2 -- 3 -- 4 -- 5 -- 6 -- 7 -- 8 -- 9 -- 10 (Ideal)

Where am I on the scale?
Why aren't I lower on the scale?
What will it take for me to get higher on the scale?

THE HASSLE TRACKER

Use this guide or your journal to begin documenting all the people, places and things you encounter in your day-to-day life that consistently make you upset. In Column 2, write down those things you typically think, feel and do in response to those things that are upsetting you. As you do this exercise, try to identify what things consistently make you upset.

Write down the people, places, and things that cause me to be upset. Record approximately when these things happen to me (Day/Time).	Record what I was thinking, feeling and doing as a consequence of the upsetting things I list in Column 1.

Table 22

P2LR STEP 2

Define and Solve Problems.

How will I solve problems I encounter when trying to change?

Ideas for Implementation

This step provides you with two different approaches to problem solving. The first approach requires that you make a list of the problems you are currently struggling with and then ask yourself a number of questions that are designed to help you think strategically about the problem, its causes, and what you need to think and do differently to address the root causes and overcome the problem.

The second approach uses what is called the "Problem Solving Planner" or PSP. This tool will guide you through a step-by-step process that helps you understand the nature and determinants of the problem before you develop a plan to address it.

1. List the most difficult problems you are currently struggling with. Problems are discrepancies between the way things are in your life and the way you want them to be.

     Problem 1:

     Problem 2:

     Problem 3:

2. How do you feel when you experience a problem?: embarrassed, guilty, angry, sad, incompetent, afraid, anxious, hopeless, unhappy, disappointed, pessimistic, frustrated, regretful, lonely, inferior, panicky, worthless.

     Problem 1:

     Problem 2:

     Problem 3:

3. What do you think or do that contributes to each problem and the negative feelings? This behavior will help you isolate those things you have control over.

     Problem 1:

     Problem 2:

     Problem 3:

4. What can you think or do differently that will help you solve the problem and eliminate the negative emotions? How will these thoughts and actions help you 1) achieve your goals, and 2) feel the way you want to feel? These

thoughts and actions should fit the valid thought system in Table__.

> Problem 1:
>
> Problem 2:
>
> Problem 3:

5. What will you do, how often, for how long? What support/resources will you need?

> Problem 1:
>
> Problem 2:
>
> Problem 3:

6. Document what you did and did not do, and how you feel as a consequence.

> Problem 1:
>
> Problem 2:
>
> Problem 3:

* Assess the rationality of your thinking by asking yourself whether or not the above thoughts and actions have been demonstrated to be effective in helping others solve the kind of problems you are trying to overcome.

The second approach you can use to implement this step relies on a problem-solving tool called the PSP. This tool has two phases.

Phase I of the PSP directs you to 1) identify the problem, 2) define it, 3) investigate to determine the causes and possible solutions, 4) decide which causes you will address and which action steps you will take to alleviate these causes, and 5) establish a schedule for monitoring progress and getting feedback that can be used to improve the strategy. In Phase II, you put the information together to make up your intervention strategy, or Problem Resolution Plan.

PSP PHASE I: Understanding the Problem

Step 1: Identify the Problem	A problem is a "gap" between what "should be" happening and what is actually happening.
Step 2: Define the Problem	Clearly stating the problem you plan to work on is essential to focus on what it is that you plan to change.
Step 3: Investigate to Determine the Causes and Possible Solutions	If you can determine what is causing the problem, then you will be able to focus your attention on the causes rather than the symptoms.
Step 4: Decide Which Causes to Address and Which Steps to Take to Alleviate Them	Once you know what the problem is, and what is causing it, you will be able to select the appropriate action steps to address each cause.
Step 5: Establish a Schedule for Monitoring Progress and Getting Feedback	You must follow up to ensure that each action step is executed.

Table 23

As indicated above, in Phase II of the PSP you put your strategy together. The matrix that follows will help you do this in a systematic way. In column 1, you list what you perceive to be the causes of the problem. In column 2, you describe the action steps you will take in connection with each cause. Finally, in column 3 you record information about when the action steps will be completed.

PSP PHASE II:
Problem Resolution Plan

Cause to Be Addressed	Action Steps	When Actions Are Completed

Table 24

P2LR STEP 3:

Develop and Implement a Resiliency Plan

What will I do to build and maintain my resilience?

Ideas for Implementation

A simple way to incorporate resiliency into your daily life is illustrated in Table 5. Because small and simple steps over time can lead to great accomplishments, using this type of a guide to set in place activities that you will do on a regularly scheduled basis to improve your resilience will, in turn, ensure that you are getting stronger and not weaker in each of the dimensions described above.

MY DAILY RESILIENCY ROUTINE

Specifically, what will I do on a daily basis to strengthen myself, when will I do it, where will I do it, and for how long will I do it?							
	Mon	Tues	Wed	Thur	Fri	Sat	Sun
Physically							
Intellectually							
Socially							
Spiritually							
Mentally & Emotionally							

Table 25

Obviously, you can use any number of formats for laying out a daily resiliency or "daily good habit" plan. There are also many tools, including SmartPhone Apps, that can help you remember your plan and document your progress. One example of a simple, yet powerful plan is provided below.

Daily Habits for Success and Increased Happiness

1. Do the things I have listed on my resiliency plan (this assumes I have a resiliency plan).

2. Set and achieve at least one new small, measurable goal each day.

3. At the end of the day, ask myself, "What went well, and what went poorly today?" For each thing that did not go well, decide what I can think and do differently to increase the likelihood that this will not happen again. If I have no control over the situation, decide what I can think that will help me feel better about it.

4. Practice being grateful for my problems. When I experience a problem think to myself, "I am grateful for the problems I experienced today because, even though they are difficult and painful, each one of them presents an opportunity for personal growth and development." After all, this statement is true. When I experience and rationally cope with problems, I become stronger. A good example of this is weight lifting. When I lift weights, the muscles being taxed send a message to my brain that causes the flexed muscles to overcompensate and grow.

5. Each time I experience a problem or difficult life event, I will think or do the following things, INSTEAD OF thinking or doing things that have upset me in the past:

6. Before going to bed, I will think of three things I can be grateful for and why.

Table 26

P2LR STEP 4:

Create a Rational Personal Vision Statement

How will I need to see myself to change or become the kind of person who consistently accomplishes these things (add elements to my RPVS)?

Ideas for Implementation

This assignment will guide you through a process of designing and testing a Rational Personal Vision Statement (RPVS) using the "Rational Personal Vision Statement Guide" and then, help you evaluate and refine your RPVS until you have decided on a final version. Once you have finalized your RPVS and identified what adds to and takes away from it, you can begin to choose to think and act in ways that will cause you to realize everything you have outlined in your final RPVS.

Over time, as you decide to make additional changes, you will most likely need to revisit this statement. This is due to the fact that a necessary first step in true change requires making sure that you vision of self, or you self-image, is aligned with the things that you want to change about yourself. Once again, this is because you can do certain things unless you become the kind of person who does those kinds of things.

There are several steps in this process:

1. Ask yourself the following "Visioning Questions" to help you begin thinking about what you want to put into your RPVS:

- What inspires me? What do I want my life to stand for?

- If I could fix one problem in the world what would it be? What would I do about this problem?

- What are my most important values?

- What are the main things that motivate me/ bring me joy and satisfaction?

- What are the two best moments I have experienced in the past 10 years?

- What three things would I do if I won a 200 million dollar lottery?

- What are my greatest strengths/abilities/traits/ things I do best?

- What are at least two things I can start doing/

do more often that use my strengths and bring me joy?

• What are at least two things I can start thinking that will bring me greater happiness?

• What are at least two things I would like to stop doing or do as little as possible?

• If a miracle occurred and my life was just as I wanted it to be, what would be different?

2. Use the "Rational Personal Vision Statement Guide" to a) identify pictures or images that represent the things you want to BEcome, Do or Get—taken together, these images will represent your ideal RPVS; b) briefly explain how each image represents something you want; c) describe the reason "WHY" you want these things; and d) after you have described what you want and WHY, decide on one "Cue Word" that represents each of the images making up your RPVS.

3. Use the "RPVS Rationality Guide" to evaluate and identify elements in your RPVS that are irrational.

4. Revise the irrational elements in your RPVS.

5. Repeat steps 2 and 3 until all elements in your RPVS are rational.

Rational Personal Vision Statement Guide

Identify 10 pictures or images that represent what you want to **BE, DO, GET**. After you have finished this step, these images will represent your Rational Personal Vision Statement. Briefly 1) explain how each image represents something you want to **BE** (calm, successful, thin, on time, confident, faithful, disciplined, fun, trustworthy, etc.), **DO** (graduate from college, get married, travel around the world, write a book, etc.) and **GET** (a new car or home, great job, a boat, etc.). Then describe the reason WHY you want the things represented by each picture. After you have described how you want to see yourself and your future, and WHY, decide on 1 "Cue-Word" that represents each of the images making up your PVS.

IMAGE 1	I want to...	The reasons WHY are...	Cue Word 1
IMAGE 2	I want to...	The reasons WHY are...	Cue Word 2
IMAGE 3	I want to...	The reasons WHY are...	Cue Word 3
IMAGE 4	I want to...	The reasons WHY are...	Cue Word 4
IMAGE 5	I want to...	The reasons WHY are...	Cue Word 5
IMAGE 6	I want to...	The reasons WHY are...	Cue Word 6
IMAGE 7	I want to...	The reasons WHY are...	Cue Word 7
IMAGE 8	I want to...	The reasons WHY are...	Cue Word 8
IMAGE 9	I want to...	The reasons WHY are...	Cue Word 9
IMAGE 10	I want to...	The reasons WHY are...	Cue Word 10
IMAGE 11	I want to...	The reasons WHY are...	Cue Word 11

Table 27

247

RPVS RATIONALITY GUIDE

Ask each element (represented by an image and cue word) in your initial Rational Personal Vision Statement (RPVS) the following questions. If you answer no to any of these questions it's likely that the element you are considering is irrational. Revise the irrational elements until you can answer yes to every question. Feel free to add to or take away from the questions provided here.

If I fully adopt this element in my Rational Personal Vision Statement, will I:
- reach my full potential?
- become the kind of person I want to be?
- achieve my short- and long-term goals?
- learn from my past, prepare for my future, and live in the present?
- have the ability to think and act in terms of principles and not emotions?
- perceive myself as someone who is in control of my destiny?
- be able to solve my problems and ask others for help when I need it?
- feel secure about who I am, and not feel insecure when others question how I see myself and live my life?
- be able to evaluate what others think and feel against my own standards, and have the courage to act according to my own convictions, regardless of what others do or say?
- feel secure enough about my beliefs that I can change them in the face of new facts?
- be able to exercise self-control by stoping, thinking, and making rational decisions?
- look beyond the surface, find real meaning, and weigh the pros and cons of an event or issue?
- wait for things that I want even when this requires patience and delaying immediate gratification?
- keep trying, even when things don't go the way I would like them to?
- see myself as someone who is equal in value to others, rather than inferior or superior, while accepting differences in my abilities, socio-economic standing, and personal potential?
- respect and obey the laws that are rational in that they are fair and just?
- respect the dignity of all men and women, without respect to religion, race, or gender?

Table 28

P2LR STEP 5:

Set Rational Goals

What are my short-, medium-, and long-term goals?

Ideas for Implementation

The purposes of Step 5 are to help you 1) begin to operationalize your Rational Personal Vision Statement (RPVS) by guiding you through the process of setting a single goal for each RPVS element; 2) evaluate the rationality of your goals; and 3) start to determine whether or not you are ready to achieve the goals you plan to set. Although the part of this step that involves assessing your readiness is somewhat redundant and may seem like "overkill," it is not. Taking a very close look at a goal before you set and start working toward the goal is key to achieving the goal. In fact, I am of the opinion that you should never set a goal that you do not plan to achieve. This process will help you decide whether the goals you set are ones that you really want to do and help you determine what it takes to achieve the goals.

Six Questions for Writing Goals:

1) Am I committed to this goal?

2) What do I plan to accomplish?

3) What will I need to do to prepare to achieve this goal?

4) When will I start and finish?

5) What barriers may I encounter when trying to achieve this goal?

6) How will I know if I succeed and achieve my goal?

1. Use the "RPVS Goal Guide" from Step 4 to write down at least one goal for each element in your RPVS. Be precise and only include goals that you are committed to and confident that you can attain. For ideas about the type, content, and format of each goal, refer to the "Six Questions for Writing Goals" listed above. In addition, refer to the questions from the Hapiness Algorithm Planner (in Section I) relating to what you need to think or do more or less of, which will help you to realize your RPVS.

2. For each goal your set using the "RPVS Goal Guide," ask the following questions:

- Do I believe I can achieve this goal?

- Do I have what it takes to achieve the goal (e.g., knowledge, skills, resources, support)?

• Based on my responses to the last question, what do I need to think or do to get what I need to accomplish each goal?

3. To assess and begin building your motivation to achieve each goal, ask yourself these questions:

• Why do I want to achieve this particular goal?

• What good things may happen if I achieve this goal?

• What bad things may happen if I do not reach this goal?

• How will things be different if I achieve this goal?

4. (a) To further assess your readiness, including how committed you are, how confident you are, and how prepared you are, you can ask yourself the following questions for each goal:

• How committed am I that I can achieve this goal? (circle number)

(no commitment) 0 -- 1 -- 2 -- 3 -- 4 -- 5 -- 6 -- 7 -- 8 -- 9 -- 10 (totally committed)

• How confident am I that I can achieve this goal? (circle number)

(no confidence) 0 -- 1 -- 2 -- 3 -- 4 -- 5 -- 6 -- 7 -- 8 -- 9 -- 10 (totally confident)

• How prepared are you to achieve this goal? (circle number)

(no preparation) 0 -- 1 -- 2 -- 3 -- 4 -- 5 -- 6 -- 7 -- 8 -- 9 -- 10 (totally prepared)

5. (b) What do you need to raise each number you circled to a 10?

6. What else do you need to achieve the goal? Improved self-image, knowledge, skills, social support, money?

RPVS GOAL GUIDE

Use this form to write down at least one goal for each element in your Rational Personal Vision Statement (RPVS). Be precise and only include goals that you are committed to, confident that you can attain, and are congruent with your RPVS.
CUE 1
CUE 2
CUE 3
CUE 4
CUE 5
CUE 6
CUE 7
CUE 8
CUE 9
CUE 10

Table 29

P2LR STEP 6:

Determine What will Motivate You to Change and Grow

What will motivate me to achieve my goals?

Ideas for Implementation

1. List and spend some time visualizing the benefits (positive outcomes) you expect to gain from making this change will motivate you and help you to remain focused on what you want to accomplish.

2. List and spend time visualizing the negative outcomes you could face if you do not make this change will motivate you and help you to remain focused on what you do want to accomplish.

3. Make a list of positive reinforcers. Things other than food and alcohol that you will reward yourself with if you do what you plan to do.

4. Use the "CCS Reinforcement Guide" to develop a plan to reinforce the goals or activities you plan to work on that

you know you will have difficulty motivating yourself to do without applying an extrinsic reward. In Column 1 list the goals you plan to reinforce. In Column 2, list subgoals or activities that will help you achieve the goal in Column. Finally, in Column 3 list the specific reinforcer that is contingent upon doing the things you listed in Column 2.

5. Evaluate your progress. If you are not doing what you plan to do, the things you have designated as reinforcers are not reinforcing. Remember, the defining characteristic of a reinforcer is that it increases the behavior it is contingent upon.

CCS REINFORCEMENT GUIDE

Goals I Plan to Reinforce	SubGoal or Goal Related Activity I Plan To Reinforce	What is the Reinforcer, How and When Will I Reinforce My Success?

Table 30

P2LR STEP 7:

Identify and Anticipate Triggers and Barriers to Change and Growth

What are the barriers to achieving my goals?

Ideas for Implementation

Use the following steps and guides to develop a plan that will help you anticipate and respond rationally to your triggers, and overcome your barriers to becoming your highest and best self. Use the information about triggers and barriers provided above to support you in this efforts.

1) Use the "Trigger Identification and Response Guide" to begin identifying and planning how you will respond to irrational triggers. In column 1, list all the people, places, and things that, when you think about or encounter them, cause you to have the urge to think or do things that are incongruent with your vision and goals. In column 2, record the things that are incongruent with your vision and goals that correspond to each trigger you listed in column 1. Finally, in column 3, list the things you can think or

do "INSTEAD OF" those things you listed in column 2. These "INSTEAD OFs" should be consistent with, and in support of, the actions you plan to take toward your vision and goals.

TRIGGER IDENTIFICATION AND RESPONSE GUIDE

Irrational triggers that cause me to think or do things that are incongruent with my vision and goals.	What have I typically thought and/or done in response to the triggers in column 1 that is inconsistent with my vision and goals?	What can I think and/or do in response to the triggers in column 1 that will be consistent with, and in support of, the actions I plan to take toward my vision and goals?

Table 31

2) Use the "Barrier Identification and Response Guide" to begin identifying and planning how you will overcome barriers to your vision, goals, and plan of action. In column

1, list all the thoughts, emotions, actions, people, places, and things that may undermine your ability to realize your vision and achieve your goals. In column 2, describe what you need to think and do to overcome each barrier you listed in column 1.

BARRIER IDENTIFICATION AND RESPONSE GUIDE

What barriers may prevent me from realizing my vision and achieving my goals?	What can I think or do to overcome the barriers I listed in column 1?

Table 32

3) Use the "RPVS Trigger and Barrier Response Planner" to begin identifying and planning how you will overcome barriers to each element in your Rational Personal Vision

Statement. In column 1, list all your RPVS cue words. In column 2, list the triggers and barriers that you anticipate in connection with each element listed in column 1. Finally, in column 3, describe what you will do to deal with each trigger and overcome each barrier listed in Column 1.

RPVS TRIGGER AND BARRIER RESPONSE PLANNER

RPVS Cue Word	Triggers and Barriers that I anticipate in connection with each RPVS element listed in column 1.	What will I think and do to deal with each trigger and overcome the barriers?
CUE 1		
CUE 2		
CUE 3		
CUE 4		
CUE 5		
CUE 6		
CUE 7		
CUE 8		
CUE 9		
CUE 10		

Table 33

P2LR STEP 8:

Create a Plan of Action

A) What will I need to think to overcome the barriers and achieve these goals?

B) What will I need to do to overcome the barriers and achieve these goals?

Ideas for Implementation

Use the "P2LR Action Planner" to develop a realistic plan that will provide you with the steps you will take to achieve your goals and realize your vision. Do this by recording all of the RPVS elements in column 1 and the goal(s) for each element in column 2. In column 3, record the possible barriers to achieving each goal and realizing each vision element. In column 4, list the specific action steps you will take to reach your goals and realize your vision. The action steps should be specific, realistic, measurable, and effective.

P2LR Action Planner

RPVS Elements	Goals	Barriers	Action Steps

Table 34

P2LR STEP 9:

Mentally Program and Internalize Your Plan of Action

How will I internalize my plan to overcome my barriers, realize my vision, and achieve my goals?

Ideas for Implementation

There are several steps you can follow to increase your abilities in these mental processes:

1. Start at conscious baseline.

2. Give yourself an assignment, with a specific objective and purpose. Set and attain goals; sort, prioritize, and solve problems; learn new skills; relax and/or remain calm under pressure; become and remain confident; make a presentation to any size group; overcome bad habits and addictions; silence your internal critic; internalize your vision and goals; answer media questions; and improve relationships. Focus on one purpose at a time.

3. Based on the assignment you give yourself, write out suggestions to "make to yourself" as you get into your relaxed state. These suggestions should be consistent with your assignment and help you stay in the "present." For example, you should use "I am" instead of "I will be" statements.

4. Create a place in your mind where you will carry out the assignment (e.g., a workshop, practice field, or resort, decompression chamber, Skillnasium).

5. Select a technique that will help you achieve your purpose.

6. Close your eyes and take time to relax (breathe) until you are ready to take on the assignment.

7. Tune inward with the initial focus on a slow relaxed

breath, while at the same time imaging that you are going into a deeper state while counting down slowly from 5, 4, 3, 2, to 1.

8. At this point, use all of your senses to work on your assignment using the suggestions you decided upon. Once again, when making suggestions use "I am" instead of "I will be" statements.

9. End your assignment with the suggestions that will bring positive benefits from this experience.

10. You are going to become alert and come out of this deeply relaxed state after counting to three: 1, 2, and 3.

11. Return to your baseline.

12. Record your progress so you can carry your accomplishments and good memories with you.

The following comments will help you better understand the process outlined above. Specifically, I provide you with some relaxation techniques and some ideas regarding how to "construct" a place in your mind. I also provide you with some visualization and creativity exercises you can use to mentally program and internalize your vision, goals, and plan of action.

Relaxed Body, Relaxed Mind

As you can see from this list of steps, one of the first things you need to do with each technique is to relax. This is because a relaxed body equates with a relaxed mind, which in turn, improves your ability to focus and attend to your self-directed visualization and imagery assignments.

Relaxation techniques typically combine breathing and focused attention to calm your body and mind. If used correctly, these techniques will help you quiet your inner critic and increase your ability to carry out your self-directed imagery assignments. In addition to amplifying the benefits of mental imagery and rehearsal, learning and applying relaxation techniques can help with a number of stress-related problems. This is documented in the U.S. National Institutes of Health, National Center for Complementary and Alternative Medicine (NCCAM) Clinical Digest, published in December 2012, which reports evidence that relaxation techniques may be an effective intervention for treating a number of stress-related disorders, including anxiety, phobias, and panic disorder; depression; headaches; lung function and asthma; immune function; heart disease and heart symptoms; hypertension; chronic insomnia; and irritable bowel syndrome.

Other reliable sources have reported evidence that relaxation may help mitigate chronic pain, fibromyalgia, premenstrual syndrome, psoriasis, and hyperactivity related to AD(H)D. The point is, investing the time to relax before using any of the following visualization techniques may have a number of benefits beyond helping you improve your rationality related to your self-image, thoughts, and behaviors.

Selecting the Right Relaxation Technique

The right technique, in the present context, is the one that suits your personal liking and helps you relax and calm your mind in preparation for completing your self-directed imagery assignment(s). Based on my experience with clients and students, the most widely studied techniques that have direct application to this step of the P2LR process are deep breathing and progressive muscle relaxation. Other effective techniques include meditation, guided imagery (similar to what is being taught in this step), self-hypnosis, yoga, Tai Chi, massage, and exercise.

The steps you should follow when using Deep Breathing and Progressive Muscle Relaxation as a means of reaching a relaxed state before doing your visualization and imagery exercise are as follows:

Deep Breathing

1. Get in a comfortable position.

2. Close your eyes.

3. Breathe in through your nose and out through your mouth.

> • As you breathe in through your nose, visualize inhaling pure oxygen that is coated with relaxation.

> • As you breathe out through your mouth, exaggerate the exhalation by visualizing blowing

out a birthday candle and imagining that you are releasing tension, stress, and strain. The exaggerated exhalation will speed up the relaxation process.

4. Continue breathing in and out until you are able to feel a sense of calm and have quieted most of the distracting thoughts (e.g., your internal critic) that may interfere with your imagery exercise.

5. Begin your visualization exercise.

Progressive Muscle Relaxation

1. Find a comfortable position.

2. Close your eyes.

3. Visualize scanning your body up and down to find an area that is "more" relaxed than most other places on your body.

4. See yourself breathing into that area (in through your nose and out through your mouth) while imagining that your inhalation is causing the "more" relaxed area to increase in diameter and your exhalation is releasing stress.

5. Do this for about 30 seconds.

6. Now visualize yourself scanning your body to find an area that is more tense than the other parts of your body. Once you have identified this area, start breathing in and

out. Once again, imagine that your inhalation is relaxing the area that is "more" tense than other areas in your body. Do this for about 30 seconds.

7. Now start tensing and relaxing muscle groups from your feet to your head while breathing in pure oxygen/relaxation and breathing out stress/tension/strain.

> • Imagine flexing the muscles in your feet for 5 seconds and then releasing. The tensing of muscles will bring blood to the area where you have flexed and will cause a sense of warmth and relaxation. Continue breathing in and out while continuing to imagine yourself taking in pure oxygen and releasing stress and strain.

> • Now flex your lower legs for 5 seconds, your calf muscles, while repeating the breathing process.

> • Next, go to your upper legs, then buttocks, abdomen, chest and back, hands, arms, shoulders, neck, and then face. Flex each muscle area for 5 seconds and then release while continuing to breathe throughout the entire process. Continue to focus on breathing in pure oxygen and exhaling all the bad things that are causing your body to tense up and feel stress.

8. After go through the muscle groups, you should be prepared to start the imagery exercise. If not, go through the process of tensing and relaxing your muscles again and

again until you are feeling calm.

9. Begin the imagery exercise.

Constructing Places in Your Mind

As I mentioned above, it is helpful to construct a "place in your mind" when you are doing your visualization work. Do not worry about how many places you build as it is estimated that humans have about 100 billion brain cells. This figure does not even include support cells, such as glial cells, that help the neurons; these have been calculated to be at least 10 times more numerous than neurons. This is to say you have plenty of real estate to work with. Furthermore, do not skimp on the quality of the places you build. Your virtual mental budget is only limited by your imagination. Once again, you can increase your commitment and intensity toward achieving your goals with things like motivational literature, pictures, images, videos, and music that are in sync with what you are trying to accomplish.

With these directions in mind, I have provided you with a number of examples of "mental places" you can create and exercises you can carry out in these places. The place I recommend that everyone learn is called a "Mental Home Movie Theater."

Mental Home Movie Theater- Create a movie theater in your mind, including seating and a screen, where you will watch yourself play out a script related to something you want to happen a certain way. Write a script and play the part. Focus on the present as if you are the character that you are watching on screen. Visualize a perfect performance until it happens and you are confident you can play the part. Follow these steps:

1. Create your theater (preferably an IMAX);

2. Write a very good, very comprehensive script. (Write a brief Script for each goal/element in your vision; Watch the Script until you believe it; and Record your progress.)

3. Get in a relaxed state (by using the breathing or muscle relaxation techniques described above).

4. Watch yourself play your part in the movie over and over again until you believe you are the character you are watching. Watch yourself reach, and achieve, your goals.

Mental Practice Room or Field- While the "Mental Movie" technique involves watching yourself play a part, this technique involves visualizing yourself practicing some activity, such as giving a speech, hitting a golf ball, calmly discussing a problem with your spouse, asking for a raise at work, eating a healthy diet, responding rationally to your common triggers. Do this by following these basic steps:

1. Get into a relaxed state.

2. Decide on a purpose.

3. Start Practicing.

Problem Room– This technique creates a place in your mind where you can store your small, medium, and large problems. The rules of this technique include the following:

1. Place all problems in this room.

2. Decide how you will determine the size and importance of the problem.

3. Organize your problems by size and importance.

4. Set a regular schedule to visit, review, and/or work on your problems.

5. In your journal, record and store successes and failures for future reference.

Problem Cards– This is one of the most effective exercises you can possibly use when you feel overwhelmed. It will help you get all of your problems out of your head and onto paper. Follow these steps to use this technique:

1. Get 3x5 cards.

2. List each of your most pressing problems on a separate card.

3. Keep your cards with you throughout the day. Also carry a pencil or pen with you.

4. Take your cards to a virtual "problem room" 2 times per day. While you are in this room, review your problems for several minutes.

5. At any time you have a thought about a problem on one of your cards, write it down on the card.

6. When the problem on a card is solved, place the card in a designated drawer in your home.

For step-by-step instructions for other mental exercises, revisit Step 9 in Section IV of this book.

P2LR STEP 10:

Observe and Master Your Internal Monologue

What will I do to keep my thoughts in support of, and aligned with, my overall plan?

Ideas for Implementation

You can implement this step by using one of the two guides that follows. I suggest that you start with the "Thought Observation and Restructuring Guide" to help you see the connection between your emotions, beliefs, and thoughts. I have divided this Guide into two parts. Part 1 helps you track and monitor your thoughts to distinguish between rational and irrational thoughts. Part 2 helps you replace irrational thoughts. After learning how to use this process, I recommend that you move on to and make a habit of using the "Life Story Restructuring Guide," as it is easier to integrate into your day-to-day life.

The Thought Observation and Restructuring Guide

Thought Observation and Restructuring Guide: Part 1

The way you think and the things you do have an impact on your emotions and sense of well-being. If you hold on to irrational beliefs (see Reference 2, which immediately follows) and/or you think negative thoughts, you will feel negative emotions (see Reference 1, which immediately follows). Consequently, to decrease your negative emotions you can replace irrational beliefs and thoughts that cause unpleasant feelings with thoughts that produce more positive emotions.

The "Thought Observation and Restructuring Guide" is designed to help you identify and replace thoughts and thought patterns that cause unpleasant emotions. Part 1 of this guide will help you monitor and evaluate your thoughts as they relate to your negative emotions. Tables A and B below are designed to help you organize yourself as you go through this thought-restructuring process.

To start the process, complete the following steps: 1) monitor your emotions throughout the day; 2) record negative emotions in column 1, Table A; 3) in column 2, record the time and context of what is going on at the time you notice the negative emotions; 4) determine which thoughts are associated with the emotions listed in column 1; 5) record negative thoughts in column 3; 6) evaluate each thought recorded in column 3 by answering the questions in column 4. Referring to the information you gathered using the "Hassle Tracker" (introduced in Step 1) should be helpful here.

Use the "Cognitive Filtering & Refinement" exercise to practice filtering out and replacing thoughts that are causing the negative emotions you record in column 1 of the "Thought Observation Guide" and ensure that your thoughts are consistent with your Rational Personal Vision Statement and goals.

After completing Table A (in Part 1), go on to Table B (in Part 2) where you will record replacement thoughts for the irrational and distorted thoughts you have recorded in Column 3, Table A.

TABLE A - Thought Record

Negative Emotions (Examples of Negative Emotions are Listed below in Reference 1) **Day/Time/Event** (When did I notice the negative emotion and what was going on around the same time?) **Related Thoughts** (The Thoughts I am thinking when I am Upset)	
Evaluate My Thoughts (These are Rules that will help me Referee my Thoughts)	
Is it Rational? (See Reference 2)	**Is it Distorted?** (See Reference 3)

Reference 1

Common Negative Emotions

Embarrassed, guilty, angry, sad, incompetent, afraid, anxious, hopeless, unhappy, disappointed, pessimistic, frustrated, regretful, lonely, inferior, panicky, worthless

Reference 2

Irrational Thinking

To sum up our definition used in Step 10, irrational thinking includes thoughts that are 1) not based on fact, 2) do not help you feel the way you want to feel, and 3) do not help you achieve your goals. To review Albert Ellis (a behavioral scientist) for purposes of this exercise, the most common irrational thoughts among Americans are as follows:

1) It is a dire necessity for me to be loved or approved by almost all others who are significant to me.

2) I must be thoroughly competent, adequate, and achieving, in all important respects in order to be worthwhile.

3) The world must be fair. People must act fairly and considerately, and if they do not, they are bad, wicked, villainous, or incredibly stupid; they should be severely blamed and punished.

4) It is awful and terrible when things are not the way I very much want them to be.

5) There is not much I can do about my anxiety, anger, depression, or unhappiness because my feelings are caused by what happens to me.

6) If something is dangerous or dreadful, I should be constantly and excessively upset about it and should dwell on the possibility of it occurring.

7) It is easier to avoid and to put off facing life's difficulties

and responsibilities than face them.

8) I'm quite dependent on others and need someone stronger than myself to rely upon; I can't run my own life.

9) My past history mainly causes my present feelings and behavior; things from my past, which once strongly influenced me, will always strongly influence me.

10) I must become very anxious, angry, or depressed over someone else's problems and disturbances if I care about that person.

11) There is a right and perfect solution to almost all problems, and it is awful not to find it.

Reference 3
Cognitive Distortions

Irrational thoughts are sometimes labeled as cognitive distortions. Cognitive distortions are patterns of thinking that produce illogical thoughts that oftentimes produce negative emotions. Once again we will review the 10 most common cognitive distortions (David Burns, Feeling Good, 1982):

1) All or Nothing Thinking - thinking in black and white when many legitimate alternatives exist.

2) Over-Generalization - pretending that everything can be judged by a single occurrence or person. Trying to "tar

everything with the same brush."

3) Mental Filter - seeing only the bad so you lose your perspective. Not widening your focus.

4) Disqualifying the Positive - As it says, this is the way the mind justifies inner-philosophies that make you unhappy.

5) Jumping to Conclusions

> (a) Mind Reader Error - assuming people think a certain thing when you have no evidence for that,

> (b) Fortune-Telling Error - assuming that a certain thing will happen when you have no evidence for that.

6) Magnification or Minimalization - blowing things out of proportion or minimalizing the good aspects in yourself or a situation.

7) Emotional Reasoning - taking things personally when they were not meant that way.

8) Should Statement - feeling things should be a certain way that you think best and letting it get to you when they are not.

9) Labeling or Mislabeling - labeling yourself or someone else, rather than seeing them for the whole person they are.

10) Personalization - thinking that things turn bad because you yourself are bad.

The Thought Observation and Restructuring Guide

Thought Observation and Restructuring Guide: Part 1

The second part of this guide is designed to systematically help you replace irrational and distorted thoughts and thought patterns. Place all of the distorted and irrational thoughts you recorded in Table A, in column 1 of Table B. 1) Decide on new thoughts you can use to counter the irrational thoughts listed in column 1; 2) list your replacement thoughts in column 2; and 3) in columns 3 and 4, respectively, develop a practice schedule for overcoming your irrational thinking. Share your progress with your therapist, if applicable.

TABLE B
"Replacement Thought" Practice Schedule

Irrational and/or Distorted Thoughts (Taken from column 3, in Table A)	
Rational Replacement Thoughts	
When and Where I Will Practice New Rational Thinking	
How Often I Will Practice	

The Life Story Restructuring Guide

Use the "Life Story Restructuring Guide" to systematically identify stories that you tell yourself that make you upset. These stories come out of irrational beliefs that undermine your goals and your rational vision of yourself and your future. They limit your potential by dictating what you can and cannot become, do, and get in life. As with the previous exercise, the way you identify these stories is by tracking and documenting what you are telling yourself when you are upset. Usually when you are upset, you are telling yourself a story that causes you to feel bad. This also means that to change your negative emotions you must edit or replace the stories that upset you with rational stories. By rational stories, I mean stories that you tell yourself that are 1) logical and consistent with known facts and reality—based on truth; 2) produce desired emotions; 3) help overcome current and future problems; 4) encourage serenity, personal growth, development, and happiness; 5) encourage learning from the past, preparing for the future, and living in the present; 6) support personal and interpersonal goals; and 7) support an optimistic view of one's self and future. Conversely, a story is irrational if it 1) is not logical and/or there is no evidence to support it as true; 2) does not help you feel the way you want to feel; 3) does not help you overcome your problems; 4) is destructive to yourself or others; and/or 5) undermines your goals.

Before you begin, you should recall Section III, which introduces Self-Sabotage. Remember, any time you attempt to change long-held beliefs, you will experience resistance. At times the negative stories you have consistently told yourself over time will re-enter your mind and cause you to feel sad and upset, even when you are attempting to feel happy and fulfilled. This incongruence will initially cause you to feel "Change-Based Cognitive Dissonance." As you will recall from what was discussed in Step 7, this type of dissonance occurs any time you think and do things that are different than things you have thought and done in the past, such as starting to exercise when you have not exercised in the past, or moving from a country where you drive on the right side of the road to a country where you drive on the left side. When this dissonance happens simply remind yourself that this is normal and healthy and that with time and persistence it will subside.

An important thing to remember here, as with other maladaptive thought-restructuring techniques, is that what you say to yourself (think) determines how you feel. And, your thoughts and feelings have an impact on your actions.

If the stories you tell yourself are upsetting, you will be upset whenever you think about these stories. If you tell yourself upsetting stories over and over again, you will undoubtedly experience a multitude of upsetting emotions like fear, discouragement, or sadness. Fortunately, because you have control over the thoughts and personal life stories you think about, you can replace or modify thoughts and the stories you tell yourself in a way that changes the way you feel. This requires a careful analysis of what is upsetting you and reframing the thoughts that are upsetting into more rational thoughts and stories.

The process for completing the "Life Story Restructuring Guide" is somewhat self-explanatory. It involves observing your emotions throughout the day until you notice that you are upset. At that point, record the story or stories you are telling yourself in column 1 of the guide. Once you have documented an irrational story in column 1, write a new script or story in column 2 that is rational. To review our definition, a rational story is 1) logical; 2) consistent with known facts and reality; 3) helps you feel the way you want to feel; 4) contributes to a Rational Self-Perception; 5) improves a sense of well-being, happiness, and serenity; 6) helps you solve your problems; and 7) helps you achieve your goals. Rehearse the script until you believe it. Finally, any time an old, irrational story crops up, replace it with the new rational story. Do this until the old story is no longer a problem.

LIFE STORY RESTRUCTURING GUIDE

Old stories You tell yourself that upset you *Irrational stories	New stories You plan to tell yourself to overcome old stories **Rational, replacement
* You can begin identifying irrational stories by noticing what you are telling yourself when you are upset. ** To be considered rational, a story must be logical, consistent with known facts and reality, help you feel the way you want to feel, contribute to and support your Rational Personal Vision, give you a sense of well-being, and help you solve your problems and achieve your goals.	

Table 35

P2LR STEP 11:

Plan to Cope Rationally.

How will I cope when I am under stress?

That is, what will I do INSTEAD OF those things I typically do when I am under a lot of stress?

Ideas for Implementation

Complete and begin implementing the "Coping Plan Matrix." This exercise will help you plan new ways of coping in response to daily stressors. If you do not think about new ways of coping in response to issues you have struggled with in the past, you will not be able to change. You simply cannot change the way you perform under stress unless you have thought about and practiced new ways of coping. This is all to say, "Failing to plan is a way of planning to fail."

COPING PLAN MATRIX

List the problems that have caused, or that I anticipate will cause, the most stress during my day/week/month.	What do I typically think and do in response to stress induced by the problem listed in column 1?	What I plan to think and/or do differently? (Ideas for replacement thoughts and actions are provided in the Appendices at the end of this section.) These new coping responses should 1) prove to be effective, 2) help me feel the way I want to feel, and 3) help me achieve my goals.

Table 36

After you have completed your new Coping Plan, practice the Anti-Flacting technique. The following diagram explains how to counteract your triggers (which were identified in Step 7) and the negative emotions they produce. Instead of reacting like you have in the past, this process can help you cope in a healthier way. The diagram reminds you to do the following: 1) breathe; 2) tell yourself you are upset; 3) tell yourself this is an opportunity to change and become stronger; and 4) tell yourself of the many things in your coping plan that you will think and do INSTEAD OF the things you have done in the past that did not work. Review this approach daily and practice using it every time you get upset.

ANTI-FLACTING

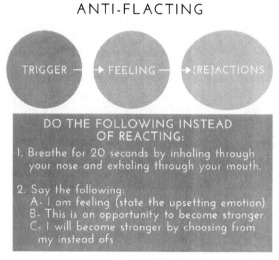

Figure 16

After reviewing the Anti-Flacting process and completing the Daily Resiliency Plan (in Step 3) and the Coping Plan described in this step (Step 11), summarize what you PLAN TO DO on a daily basis in the following "Daily Routine & Coping Matrix" below. Be specific. Carry this guide with you at all times. Review the guide every morning and night. Use column 3 to record your successes and failures. Use this feedback to refine and improve your plans.

DAILY ROUTINE & COPING MATRIX

Day of Week	Routine (What I Will Do Today)	Feedback (What did I do to change and to improve my performance?)
Monday		
Tuesday		
Wednesday		
Thursday		
Friday		
Saturday		
Sunday		
Coping Thoughts and Actions		
What rational things will I think when I experience stress and temptation?	What rational things will I do when I experience stress and temptation?	

Table 37

P2LR STEP 12:

Evaluate Your Progress and Adjust Your Plan of Action

How will I track my progress and make necessary adjustments to ensure my success?

Ideas for Implementation

The following ideas will help you develop a plan for determining how you are doing and what you need to change to improve your performance. Essentially, this involves asking yourself questions that provide you insight into whether or not you are doing what you plan to think and do to achieve your goals. You may want to routinely ask yourself these specific questions:

- Am I making progress toward my goal?
- What am I doing that is going well and why?
- What am I doing that is not working and why?
- What could I do better with a little tweaking?
- What should I stop doing so I can do other things?
- Where is my time most being wasted?

- What discipline do I most need to implement into my day?
- What drains my energy just to think about doing again?
- What changes do I need to make?

Another set of questions focuses specifically on what you should THINK or DO more or less of to improve. You may want to refer back to the Happiness Algorithm Planner (HAP) you filled out in Section I to answer these questions:

- What do I need to think more about to achieve this goal?
- What do I need to think less about to achieve this goal?
- What do I need to do more of to achieve this goal?
- What do I need to do less of to achieve this goal?
- Where do I need to spend more time?
- Where do I need to spend less time?
- With whom should I spend more time?
- With whom should I spend less time?
- What will prevent me from thinking and doing these things (knowledge, skills, motivation)?
- Who may prevent me from doing these things?

Finally, use the "Evaluation Planning Guide" as a model for developing a system to track and document your progress

(Cole, 1999). In column 1, list the goals you plan to track with this guide. In column 2, record the action steps you plan to carry out to achieve each goal. In column 3, describe how you will know whether or not you can carry out each action step and achieve your goals. Lastly, in column 4, document your successes and failures. When you document failures, record what you plan to think or do differently to get back on track toward your goals.

P2LR Evaluation Planning Guide

What Goals Do I Plan to Track?	
What Action Steps Do I Plan to Track?	
How Will I Know if I Carry Out My Action Steps and Achieve My Goals? (My Performance Standards)	
What Will I Think or Do Differently to Overcome My Failures?	

Table 38

Finally, before moving onto the next Quick Start, you may want to summarize your thinking in response to the above questions into a single cohesive plan. You can do this using the following table. As with all of the tables provided throughout the book, you may want to simply transfer this information to your journal to provide for more space.

P2LR Prompt Question:

"What do you want to change or improve in my life?"

P2LR Quick Start Questions	My Ideas For Implementing Each Step
1) How will I keep track of how I am doing relative to what I am trying to change or improve?	
2) How will I solve problems that I encounter when trying to change?	
3) What will I do to build and maintain my resilience?	
4) How will I need to see myself to change or become the kind of person who consistently accomplishes these things (add elements to my RPVS)?	
5) What are my short-, medium-, and long-term goals?	

Table 39

P2LR Quick Start Questions	My Ideas For Implementing Each Step
6) What will motivate me to achieve my goals?	
7) What are the barriers to achieving my goals?	
8) A) What will I need to think to overcome the barriers and achieve these goals? B) What will I need to do to overcome the barriers and achieve these goals?	
9) How will I internalize my plan to overcome my barriers, realize my vision, and achieve my goals?	
10) What will I do to keep my thoughts in support of, and aligned with, my plan?	

Table 39

P2LR Quick Start Questions	My Ideas For Implementing Each Step
11) How will I cope when I am under stress?	
12) How will I track my progress and make necessary adjustments to ensure my success?	

Table 39

QUICK START 2
THE PERSONAL ENHANCEMENT PLANNER

Quick Start 2 is a guide that you can use to set up an abbreviated plan to change or improve. This approach, referred to here as the Personal Enhancement Planner (PEP), guides you through a number of steps that incorporate and integrate the P2LR process. As you respond to each step, you will be developing a plan that you will use, on a day-to-day basis, to help you remember exactly what you plan to change and how you plan to maintain the change, including how you will identify triggers, overcome barriers, and achieve your most important goals.

A) Determine What You Want to Change

Self-improvement requires changing your behavior by either 1) adding a positive behavior like exercise, or 2) eliminating a negative behavior like oversleeping. To begin self-improvement, select the behavior you want to change.

B) Make a Commitment to Yourself by Writing a Change Goal

I will (describe the behavior you plan to add or eliminate)

on or before (date by which you will have maintained this change for at least 21 days) _____. I will begin preparing for this change on _____. I will have completed my preparation by _____. I will begin changing on (date) _____.

C) Prepare to Change

List the things you need to begin and maintain the change. These items include obtaining information (from a credible source), skills, resources (equipment, food, books), permission, etc. Also, list where or from whom you will get these things, and when you will get them. If possible, interview someone, read a book about someone, or watch a movie about someone who made a similar change.

- What do I need?
- Where or from whom will I get what I need?
- When will I get these things?

D) Develop Your First Plan for Change

List the steps (small, realistic, achievable) for improvement. Also indicate when you will take these steps (e.g., several times a day, daily, or weekly).

- What will I do?

- When will I do it?

E) Get Support For Change

Although the change process is ultimately your responsibility, it can be very helpful to get support from others. Ask one or more people to help you improve. Those who agree to participate should read and sign your improvement strategy.

1) I (name of supporter) _____
_____, agree to provide support and encouragement

to (your name) _____, in his or her efforts to make the change described above. My support will include: _____.

2) I (name of supporter) _____ _____, agree to provide support and encouragement to (your name)_____, in his or her efforts to make the change described above. My support will include:_____.

F) Plan to Reward Yourself When You Make Changes

Rewarding your changes can help you maintain the change. Develop a list of rewards (that are inexpensive and unrelated to food or drugs/alcohol) that you can treat yourself to upon completing each step in your improvement process. Indicate when you will get rewards and under what conditions.

G) Visualize and List the Benefits of Making This Change

Visualizing the benefits (positive outcomes) you expect to gain from making this change will motivate you and help you to remain focused on what you want to accomplish. List these benefits here.

H) Visualize and List the Negative Consequences of Not Making This Change

Visualizing the negative outcomes you could face if you do not make this change will motivate you and help you to remain focused on what you do want to accomplish. List these possible negative outcomes here.

I) Anticipate and List the Obstacles to Making This Change, and What You Can Do to Overcome Them

Anticipating and developing strategies to overcome obstacles can help you avoid setbacks. List thoughts, behaviors, or excuses that may be barriers to making this change. Also, list external barriers (people, places, things) that may stand in the way of your improvement.

J) Determine and List Those Things in Your Life That You Need to Alter About Yourself or Your Environment to Make the Change

K) *Write a Daily Routine for Change*

Every day, begin your self-improvement process by doing the following:

1) Visualize the benefits you will get from changing, and the negative consequences if you do not change.

2) Review barriers you may encounter and strategies you will use to overcome them.

3) Review the steps listed in your PEP change strategy and then list those steps you will take action on today (you can list these items on a 3x5 Daily Action Card you can carry with you throughout the day).

4) Follow through consistently and repetitively on the steps you listed on your Daily Action Card.

5) After the change process begins, become aware of unforeseen things that impede your progress; record these in your journal as they come up, along with strategies for countering them.

6) When faced with barriers, counter them.

7) Track your progress by keeping a daily log where you record your daily successes, failures and strategies for overcoming them, insights and lessons learned, and so on **(Emphasize Your Successes)**; if your improvement plan is not working, make appropriate modifications until you "get it right"; successful change may require a number of modifications in your approach.

ABOUT THE AUTHOR

Dr. Galen E. Cole, Ph.D., M.P.H., LPC, DAPA, BCPC, GA-CADC-III, has extensive training and experience in counseling psychology, psychiatric epidemiology, behavioral science research, entertainment education, mass and interpersonal communication, and public health. As a psychotherapist, he sees clients out of three offices in the Atlanta-metro area. As a population health professional, he has worked as a behavioral scientist and director of research and evaluation activities in various centers, institutes, and offices at the U.S. Centers for Disease Control and Prevention (CDC) in Atlanta, Georgia, where he now serves as Associate Director for Communication Science in the Division of Cancer Prevention and Control.

Dr. Cole has taught counseling psychology, equine-assisted mental health, behavioral and evaluation research, and a number of other counseling and health-related courses at the university level. He has been on the faculty at Northern Arizona University, Arizona State University, University of Idaho, Pennsylvania State University, and is currently an adjunct member of the graduate faculty at the Rollins School of Public Health at Emory University in Atlanta, Georgia. Dr. Cole has extensive experience practicing what he teaches, including working on staff and as a consultant at numerous clinics, hospitals, and community-based organizations; serving as the executive director of a not-for-profit foundation; working as an assistant director of public health in Phoenix, Arizona; and consulting with numerous national and international organizations including the United Nations Children's Fund (UNICEF), the Pan American Health Organization (PAHO), the World Bank, and the World Health Organization (WHO).

Dr. Cole was appointed by the Governor of Georgia to serve on the Georgia Human Resources (DHR) Board. In this capacity, he served as chair of the DHR committee that provides policy guidance to the state Division of Mental Health, Developmental Disabilities, and Addictive Diseases. He has also received distinguished alumni awards from two of the universities he attended. Dr. Cole has been a trainer and consultant in the Central Asian Republics, Nigeria, China, Thailand, Kenya, Switzerland, Australia, Peru, Germany, Uganda, and the Middle East, where he has conducted training with the Palestinian Health Authority and the Israeli Ministry of Health. He has been widely published and has made presentations at conferences and training seminars across the world. Dr. Cole and his wife, Priscilla, have been married for over thirty-eight years and are the parents of five children and the grandparents of five grandchildren.

References

ABBATANGELO-GRAY, J., COLE, G. E., & KENNEDY, M. G. (2007). Guidance for evaluating mass communication health initiatives: Summary of an expert panel sponsored by the Centers for Disease Control and Prevention, Evaluation & The Health Professions, Vo. 30, No. 3, pp. 229-253.

BALCAZAR, H., HARTNER, J. & COLE, G. E., (1993). The effects of prenatal care utilization and maternal risk factors on pregnancy outcome between Mexican Americans and Non-Hispanic Whites. Journal of the National Medical Association, Vol. 85, No. 3, pp. 195-202.

BALACAZAR, H., COLE, G. E. & HARTNER, J. (1992). Mexican Americans use of prenatal care and its relationship to maternal risk factors and pregnancy outcome. American Journal of Preventive Medicine, Vol. 8, No. 1, pp. 1-7.

BELLOC, N.B., & BRESLOW, L. (1972). Relationship of physical health status and health practices. Preventive Medicine, Vol. 1, pp. 409–421.
BURNS, D. D. (1980) Feeling Good: The New Mood Therapy. Avon Books.

CAUTELA, J.R., & KASTENBAUM, R. (1967). A reinforcer survey schedule for use in therapy, training, and research. Psychological Reports, 20, pp. 1115-1130.

CAUTELA, J.R. (1983). The self-control triad: description and clinical applications. Behavior Modification, 7, pp. 299-315.

CHERVIN, D., NOWAK, G., & COLE, G. E. (1999). Using audience research in designing public health initiatives at the federal level. Social Marketing Quarterly, Vo. 5, No. 3, pp. 34-39.

COLE, G., FRIEDMAN, G., & BAGWELL, M. (1986). A worksite behavioral health education program based on operant conditioning. Occupational Health Nursing, 24(3), pp. 132-137.

COLE, G. E., WALDRON, S. (2010). Precious Time: The Psychology of Effective Parenting With Parenting Plans. Circle C Publishing, Atlanta, GA.

COLE, G. E. (1999). Advancing The Development and Application of Theory-Based Evaluation in the Practice of Public Health. American Journal of Evaluation, Vo. 20, No. 3, pp. 453-470.

COLE, G. E., LEONARD, B., HAMMOND, S. & FRIDINGER, F. (1998). Using Stages of Behavioral Change constructs to measure the short-term effects of a worksite-based intervention to increase moderate physical activity. Psychological Reports, No. 82, pp. 615-618.

COLE, G. E., POGOSTIN, C., WESTOVER, B., RIOS, N. & COLLIER, C. (1995). Addressing problems in evaluating health-relevant programs through a systematic planning and evaluation model. Risk: Issues in Health, Safety and Environment , Vol. 6, No. 1, pp. 37-57.

COLE, G. E., HOLTGRAVE, D. & RIOS, N. (1993). Systematic development of trans-theoretically based behavioral risk management programs. Risk: Issues in Health, Safety and Environment , Vol. 4, No. 1, pp. 67-93.

COLE, G. E., TIMMRECK, T., PAGE, R. & WOODS, S. (1992). Patterns and prevalence of substance use among Navajo youth. Health Values, Vol. 16, No. 3, pp. 50-57.

COLE, G. E., WALLACE, J. & MCCARTAN, D. (1991). An assessment of the impact of indoor air quality on employee health and satisfaction levels. Occupational Health and Safety, May, pp. 38-51.

COLE, G. E., TUCKER, L. & FRIEDMAN, G. (1990). Relationships among measures of alcohol drinking behavior, life-events and perceived stress. Psychological

Reports, Vol. 67, pp. 587-591.

COLE, G. E., TUCKER, L. & FRIEDMAN, G. (1987). Absenteeism data as a measure of cost effectiveness of stress management programs. American Journal of Health Promotion, Vol. 1, No. 4, pp. 12-15.

COLE, G. E., EDDY, J. & FRIEDMAN, G. (1987). A protocol for selecting quality worksite health enhancement services and programs. Occupational Health and Safety, Vol. 56, No. 4, pp. 30-34.

COLE, G. E., TUCKER, L. & FRIEDMAN, G. (1986). Measures of objective and subjective stress by level of income. Psychological Reports, Vol. 59, pp. 139-142.

COLE, G. E., DUNCAN, D. & FRIEDMAN, G. (1986). A systems perspective for hospital based health promotion. Optimal Health, Vol. 3, No. 2, pp. 24-27.

COLE, G. E., FRIEDMAN, G. & BAGWELL, M. (1986). A worksite behavioral health education program based on operant conditioning. Occupational Health Nursing,Vol. 24, No. 3, pp. 132-137.

COLE, G. E. (1985). Life change events as stressors and their relationship to mental health among undergraduate university students. Psychological Reports, Vol.56., pp. 387-390.

COLE, G. E. (1984). Articulating health promotion into a health services administration curriculum. Health Matrix, Vol. 2, pp. 80-81.

COLE, G. E. (2006). Communication Surveillance: A Case for Message Testing and Information Surveillance in Proactive Risk Communication. G7i Workshop on Proactive Risk Communication (May 2-3, 2006), Berlin, Germany.
COLE, G. & PRUE, C. (1999). CDCynergy: Tool for Strategically Planning Health Communication. 127th Annual Meeting of the American Public Health Association (1999). Chicago, IL.

COVELLO, V. T. (2003). Best Practices in Public Health Risk and Crisis Communication. Journal of Health Communication. Sup. 1: pp. 5-8.

DEINER, E. (2000). Subjective well-being: The science of happiness and a proposal for a national index. American Psychologist, Vol 55(1), pp. 34-43

ELLIS, A., HARPER, R. A. & POWERS, M. (1975). A New Guide to Rational Living.

FISHBEIN, M., BANDURA, A., TRIANDIS, H.C., KAUFER, F.H., & BECKER, M.H. (1991). Factors influencing behavior and behavior change. Final report prepared for NIMH theorists workshop, Washington, D.C.

FORDYCE, M. W. (2005) A Review of Research on the Happiness Measures: A Sixty Second Index of Happiness and Mental Health. Social Indicators Research Series, V 26, pp. 373-399.

FREIMUTH, V., COLE, G. E. & KIRBY, S. (2001). Issues in Evaluating Mass-Mediated Health Communication Campaigns in Evaluation in Health Promotion: Principles and Perspectives. WHO Regional Publications, European Series; No 92, pp. 475-492.

GRAHAM, C (2009). Happiness Around the World: The Paradox of Happy Peasants and Miserable Millionaires", OUP Oxford.

GREENBERG, B., SALMON, C., PATEL, D., BECK, V. & COLE, G. E. (2004). Evolution of an Entertainment Education Research Agenda in Cody, M.J., Singhal, A., Sabido, M., & Rogers, E.M. (Eds.) Entertainment-Education Worldwide: History, Research, and Practice. Lawrence Erlbaum Associates, Publishers, Mahwah, NJ.

GOTTMAN, J. (1995). Why Marriages Succeed or Fail: And How You Can Make Yours Last.

LOFLAND, D. (1998). Thought Viruses: Powerful Ways to Change Your Thought Patterns and Get What You Want in Life.

LOSADA, M. & HEAPHY, E. (2004). The role of positivity and connectivity in the performance of business teams: A nonlinear dynamics model. American Behavioral Scientist, Vol. 47, No. 6, pp. 740-765.

MCMAHON, D. M. (2004). The History of Happiness: 400 B.C. – A.D. 1780, Daedalus Journal, Spring. PAGE, R., COLE, G. E., & TIMMRECK, T. (1994). Basic Epidemiological Methods and Biostatistics. Jones & Bartlett Publishers, Boston, MA.

PAGE, R. & COLE, G. E. (1992). Demoralization and Living Alone: Outcomes from an Urban Community Study. Psychological Reports, Vol. 70, pp. 275-280.

PAGE, R. & COLE, G. E. (1991). Loneliness and alcoholism risk in late adolescence: A comparative study of adults and adolescents. Adolescence, Vol. 26, N. 104, pp. 925-930.

PAGE, R. & COLE, G. E. (1991). Demographic predictors of self-reported loneliness in adults. Psychological Reports, Vol. 68, pp. 938-945.

PAGE, R. & COLE, G. E. (1986). School health education: A nation at risk. Wellness Perspectives, Vol. 3, No. 2, pp. 37-38.

PAGE, R., WRYE, S. & COLE, G. E. (1986). The role of loneliness in health and wellness. Home Healthcare Nursing, Vol. 4, No. 1, pp. 6-10.

PAGE, R. & COLE, G. E. (1985). Fishbein's Model of Behavioral Intentions: A framework for health education research and development. Int'l Quarterly of Community Health Education, Vol. 5, No. 4, pp. 321-329.

PREMACK, D. (1965). Reinforcement theory. In D. Levin (Ed.), Nebraska Symposium on Motivation. Lincoln, Nebraska: University of Nebraska Press, pp. 123-180.

RATH, T., & HARTER, J. K. (2010). Wellbeing: The Five Essential Elements. Based on The Gallup-Healthways Well-Being Index.
ROBLES, R., COLON, H., DIAZ, N., MACGOWEN, R., CANCEL, L. & COLE, G. E. (1994). Behavioral risk factors and HIV infection of injection drug users at detoxification clinics in Puerto Rico. International Journal of Epidemiology, Vol. 23, No. 3, pp. 595-601.

SELIGMAN, M. E. P. (2012). Flourish: A Visionary New Understanding of Happiness and Well-being.

SELIGMAN, M.E.P. (2004). Can Happiness be Taught?. Daedalus Journal, Spring.

SALMON, C., WOOTEN, K., GENTRY, E., COLE, G. E. & KROGER, F. (1996). AIDS Knowledge Gaps: Results from the first decade of the epidemic and implications for future public information efforts. Journal of Health Communication, Vol. 1, No. 2, pp. 141-155.

SKINNER, B.F. (1953). Science of self-control. New York: Holt, Rinehart & Winston, Inc.

THOMAS, S., COLE, G. E., CROUSE-QUIN, S. & FREIMUTH, V. (2001). A descriptive comparison between blacks and whites on attitudes towards health research and researchers, and perceived knowledge of the Tuskegee Syphilis Study, Social Science and Medicine,Vo. 52, pp. 797-808.

THE SEATTLE AREA HAPPINESS INITIATIVE (2011): The Happiness Initiative All Rights Reserved, http://wholelifewellbeing.com.

TIMMRECK, T. & COLE, G. E. (1989). Health services administration skills: An overlooked need of community health education and health promotion. Health Education, Feb/March, pp. 36-43.
TIMMRECK, T. COLE, G. E., JAMES, G. & BUTTERWORTH, D. (1987). The health education and health promotion movement: A theoretical jungle. Health Education, October/November, pp. 24-28.

TUCKER, L., COLE, G. E. & FRIEDMAN, G. (1987). Stress and serum cholesterol: A study of 7,000 adult males. Health Values, Vol. 2, No. 3, pp. 34-39.

TUCKER, L., COLE, G. E. & FRIEDMAN, G. (1986). Physical fitness: A buffer against stress. Perceptual and Motor Skills, Vol. 63, pp. 955-961.
WALLIS, C. (2005). "Science of Happiness: New Research on Mood, Satisfaction". TIME.

WEED, S. (2013). AAEGIS International: The Character Education Company. www.aegis-character. com.

WILKES, M., SRINVASAN, M., COLE, G. E., TARDIF, R., RICHARDSON, L. & PLESCIA, M. (2012). Discussing Uncertainty and Risk in Primary Care: Recommendations of a Multi-Disciplinary CDC Panel Regarding Communication around Prostate Cancer Screening, Journal of General Internal Medicine (in press).

CPSIA information can be obtained
at www.ICGtesting.com
Printed in the USA
FFOW02n0857021115
18249FF